Prophetic Gatekeepers

Prophetic Gatekeepers

Intercessional Decrees & Declarations

Ora Holloway

Prophetic Gatekeepers
Intercessional Decrees and Declarations by Ora Holloway

Cover Design by Susanne Alsaraf

Unless otherwise indicated, all scriptural quotations are from the King James Version of the Holy Bible. Copyright @ 1979, 1980, 1982 by Thomas Nelson Inc.

This book was printed in the United States of America.

To order additional copies of this book, contact:
Xlibris Corporation
1-888-795-4274
www.Xlibris.com
Orders@Xlibris.com
53663

CONTENTS

Introduction

This book began to take form as I was sitting at my computer, preparing to write a prayer decree for our Friday night prayer meeting. The words continued to come to my mind. I began to write from my personal experience regarding the gift of Prophetic intercession. Prophetic intercession is written from the perspective of an intercessor who has a prophetic anointing. Those who are able to hear the voice of God. To hear God's voice is a built-in desire not only for intercessors but people in general. Many people hear the voice of God, but just don't recognize that He is speaking. They say things like something told me to do this or that. I felt I should have done it this way or that. These are nudging that God is trying to get our attention and train us how to listen to our inner spirit.

My heart's desire is that those reading this book will come into a greater understanding of how to listen and become in tune with God's voice. We hear God through the various avenues such as prompting, nudging, tugging, burden, weeping, laughter our inner spirit and most of all through His written word.

Waiting patiently is the key to hearing from God. On rare occasion would we hear Him speak as we do. He speak from the inner voice of our spirit, that will say, I should have done that. He doesn't always speak as soon as we make a request and begin to talk. This is the time I believe when the fruit of patience must take root in our heart and produce its fruit. Don't run off and leave the Holy Spirit. Wait upon the Lord for his interpretation of your prayers, prophecy, and dreams. If He doesn't answer you tonight, go back the next night and wait, He will answer.

May this book teach you servitude and respect for the gifts and callings God has placed upon your life.

Yours in Christ,
Ora Holloway
Joliet, Illinois

Chapter 1

THE WORKINGS OF PROPHETIC GATEKEEPERS

*I will stand at my watch and station myself on the ramparts; I
will look to see what he will say to me, and what answer I am
to give to this complaint.*

—Habakkuk 2:1

In this book intercessors are also known as gatekeepers, watchman and
porters. Every intercessor must develop the ability to wait before God for
revealed answers and act accordingly.

Who are gatekeepers? Gatekeepers are individuals who have been
entrusted with the keys and secrets of God revelation, wisdom, knowledge
and authority to get the job done. Jesus said, and I will give unto thee the
keys of the Kingdom of Heaven and whatsoever thou shall bind on earth
shall be bound in heaven and whatsoever thou shall loose on earth shall be
loosed in Heaven, Mat. 16:19.

Therefore, gatekeepers/intercessors has the power to loose things from
Heaven and release them into the earth. The keys represent authority and
divine ability which God has given intercessors to unlock spiritual gates.
Gatekeepers are God's ambassadors which has the ability to open gates
that will bring change and affect the destiny of the world bring them
into alignment with God's Kingdom purpose. Did you not know that
there are various kind of gatekeepers. There are intercessor gatekeepers,
worship gatekeepers that will bring in the presence of God, pioneer or

apostolic gatekeepers that will open new grounds or places in the spirit before they are manifested in the earth realm, prophetic gatekeepers to decree, declare, proclaim and things that are invisible to come forth in the natural.

Gatekeepers have a guardian anointing they guard their post with care. What do they guard? Gatekeepers guard, protect, watch monitor and stop unwanted entrance through gates. In the Old testament gates was the place where the Elders of the city would come to make decisions and settle disputes. Those decisions affected the lives and destiny of those under the Elder's authority. It is our function as gatekeepers in the Body of Christ to guard the holy things of God, to protect, watch, monitor and stop unwanted entrance of things from coming into the house of God and into the earth realm. We have a great responsible as intercessors. God values your job assignment as a intercessor/gatekeeper and know that your work will not go unrewarded.

Purpose of gates:

- Gates are places of access Nehemiah 7:3.
- Gates are places of observation-the watchman saw another man running and he call down to the gatekeeper on the wall, 2 Sam. 18:26.
- Gates are places of worship, 1 Chronicles 9:33.
- Gates are places of public assembly, Esther 2:21.
- Gates are places of transformation, Esther 4:1-2.
- Gates are places of prayer, watching, prophetic revelation and outpouring, Habakkuk 2:1-3.
- Gates are places of where spiritual battles are won or lost, Judges 5:12.

God showed Habakkuk the evil that was taking place during his lifetime. It seem as though God wasn't moving quick enough for Habakkuk. He wanted an answer to the problem right then and there. Sometime the answers to our request are not granted as soon as they are received. During these times I believe God stands back to see what will be our next step. Will we hold on and remain faithful in prayer or will we give up and say forget it, I'll do it myself. Most time we get into trouble and come back to God later crying to Him to fix the situation when we should have remain steadfast in the first place and develop some patience.

How long, Oh Lord will I call for help and you will not hear, Habakkuk asked? I cry out unto thee of violence and thou wilt not save. Habakkuk reminded God that it was He who gave him the vision concerning the violence and injustice going on during his lifetime and that God wasn't doing anything about it. After he laid down his complaining, he said, "I will stand my watch and set myself on the rampart and watch to see what He (God) will say to me and the Lord answered me and said; write the vision and make it plain on tablets, that he may run who reads it. For the vision is yet for an appointed time, but at the end it will speak, and it will not lie. though it tarries, wait for it because it will surely come and will not tarry"(Hab. 2:1-3).

Habakkuk said I will stand, watch, make myself steady and listen to what God has to say regarding my complaint. I position myself to hear from God. When we have prayed about a situation the next thing to do is what Habakkuk did, position yourself and that involved waiting before God for the answer. Position yourself in prayer, reading the word and have some quiet time in His presence. Too many times we stop praying and waiting in His presence before we receive the answer to our prayers. Habakkuk, the watchman, was given the vision from God and was instructed to report what he saw (Habakkuk 2:1).

The Prophet as a watchman may be called upon to preach to the people and declare what God has said or what they see, (Isaiah 21:6, Ezek. 33:7). He does this by unction and power of the Holy Spirit and not of his own intellect or feeling. we must remember that the mouth of the watchman is a weapon. It can be used for good or much bad. Jesus said the words we speak are alive. Habakkuk was given his assignment by God and was held accountable to God for its completion. We must not be side tracked by what others say but keep a listening ear to the heart of God and move when He says move.

What is prophetic intercession?

Prophetic intercession is a partner relationship between you and God. Prophetic intercession involves praying, receiving, releasing and petitioning God on behalf of others. It's responding to the Holy Spirit's prompting in faith and obedience. It's a commitment to praying through God's prophetic purpose. In addition, it is the ability to pray and intercede with prophetic insight empowered by God's Spirit regarding specific issues, situations and concerns God brings to mind. In this ministry you become a laborer together with God and enter into a partnership with the Almighty to fulfill divine purpose.

Who are prophetic intercessors/gatekeepers?

Responsibilities

When we speak of prophetic intercessor, we're speaking of a prophet who has an intercession anointing or an intercessor who prophesy with a prophetic edge. Prophetic intercessors has more deeper prayers then intercessors. They can flow in prophetic anointing and they have a keener discerning when it comes to things in the realm of the spirit. Prophetic intercessors must be secure in this office because at times they'll see and hear things in the spirit that might seem as though they are off course and missed the mark. Jonah experience this when God sent him on an assignment to tell the people of Nineveh the city was going to be destroyed. The people of Nineveh heard the message and turned to God and Judgment was postponed. God chose to show mercy. Because judgment was postponed it seem as though Jonah lied because it didn't come to pass. Remember God will always show mercy when people show a change of heart.

Jonah was highly upset because God stayed His hand of judgment and extended His mercy. Jonah should have been filled with joy that God's hand of mercy was shown, but he wasn't. He was very angry. He had the wrong attitude. We must be careful that our attitudes doesn't get the better of us. I ask you, where was the compassion of the prophet? On himself. Jonah was more concerned about his ego than the lives of many people being destroyed. God has no pleasure in the death of the wicked (Ezekiel 33:11), that means intercessor must be sensitive to change, compassionate, merciful and able to shift in responding to a change of plan when God directs. Our job is to be flexible and obedient to the directive of God, not to do His job for Him. For God always sees the big picture in every situation.

Knowing the prophetic intercession ministry

The prophetic intercession ministry has many purposes but the primary one is to release the will of God into the earth realm. It is the joining of the prayer, gift of revelation, word of knowledge that is brought into the prayer room to pray His will on earth as it is willed in Heaven. Therefore, staying connected to the throne room is a must.

Purpose

1. Prophetic intercessors has the ability to receive instant prayer request from the prompting of the Spirit of God that should be prayed about until the burden is lifted. Prophetic intercession often times comes with instruction, direction, guidance, confirmation and warning in unseen situations and circumstances.

2. Prophetic intercession is waiting before God in order to hear or to receive God's burden, His Word, His concern, His directive, His vision or His promises then responding back to the Lord and or to the people with appropriate actions or instructions. When operating in prophetic intercession there maybe times of weeping and travailing. Sometime one may experience pain in our body. There are burdens given for an immediate response and there are others you will carry with you over a period of time. When you have God's heart you will begin to experience brokenness because now you're connecting with the purposes of God's heart (Luke 2:36-38).

3. Prophetic intercession can come in the form of a sudden urge of a prayer burden, prayer prompting, strong crying certain feeling of sadness flowing deep within. I have experience sometime feeling hungry, but not for food. It's God way of interrupting our schedule and stepping into man's situation to alter certain situations for another person.

4. Prophetic intercession paves the way for the fulfillment of the promises and prayer requests. Prophetic intercession is an urgency or pulling in one's spirit to pray, given by the Holy Spirit for situations or circumstances with which you have little knowledge of the natural. When we do this, we begin to pray requests that are on the heart of God. Surely the Sovereign Lord does nothing without revealing His plan to his servants the prophet (Amos 3:7).

5. Prophetic intercession includes intercession and prophecy. One author said that a prophetic intercessor has his ear in heaven hearing God and his mouth on earth declaring God's will. As he prays what the Holy Spirit reveals, God's will release it in the earth.

6. Prophetic intercession is where the anointing of the prophet and priest merge together pleads with God for situations and circumstances to fulfill God's divine purpose and will. If they are prophets and have the word of the Lord, let them plead with the Lord Almighty (Jeremiah 27:18).

Prophetic intercession soon became a strong part of my personal life. One member asked that I pray with her regarding a stolen check. I prayed and the prophetic word was you shall receive it about Friday of that week. I spoke what I heard in my spirit. When I saw her again she said the check was returned, praise God. That's what I'm talking about. Having a situation, telling it to God and in turn he gives you the answer, just like that. Prophetic intercessors who are faithful to praying will soon began to receive regular answers to their prayers and eventually move into prophetic intercession where they would begin to hear more clearly God's directive.

Chapter 2

HOW TO MOVE IN PROPHETIC INTERCESSION

First and foremost in order to move in prophetic intercession your spirit, heart and motive must be right to move effectively. And truth must be your foundation and pure worship from the heart in order to connect our hearts with God. As intercessors we must get in a place of worship where our spirit commune with the Father and we move from the flesh realm to the spirit realm. Worship is not about how the presence of God falls on you it's not how wonderful you can sing or pray. It's not about impressing others, but it's about our spirit being connected to the heart of God, this gives you the ability to hear what He is saying. Worship is about bowing in submission before God. He is searching for true worshippers.

> The hour cometh and now is when the true worshippers shall worship the Father in Spirit and Truth for the Father seeketh such to worship Him John (4:23-24).

The Father is seeking believers who will worship from their born-again spirit instead of an intellectual knowing. Intercession should begin with a heart filled with praise and thanksgiving. The Psalmist said, "Let us come before His presence with thanksgiving and enter into His court with praise". When we praise God it then lead one to a place of worship. According to the Americana International Encyclopedia, worship is defined as giving honors to a divine God, to acknowledge His worthiness. Words addressed to Him, either said or sung to acknowledge His acts and greatness.

Worship is a stirring in your spirit where we began to feel His presence and find ourselves seated in the throne room of heaven in a place where we are no longer concerned about your surrounding but basking in the presence. The definition for worship in Hebrew is Shachah meaning to prostrate, to bow or fall down, in submission as to pay homage. The Psalmist said, "O come, let us worship and bow down; let us kneel before the Lord our Maker." It's sad to say, but we are living in a time when are trying to worship Father, without being connected to Him. God is a Spirit. No one is able to truly worship God in Spirit without being born of His Spirit.

> Jesus said, 'except a man be born of water and of the Spirit, he cannot enter the Kingdom of God. They that are born after the flesh is flesh and they that are born after the spirit is spirit" (1 John 3:5, 6).

Jesus is saying we were born of the flesh (human birth) and flesh will never connect with the Spirit of God without being born anew, at best we will only produce fleshly worship exciting the emotions of man, but not producing any real changes. This is like trying to mix oil and water no matter how you stir it they will never come together. Jesus said to Nicodemus you must be born again from above if you wish to communicate with God. We communicate with the world through the body through the avenue of our five senses, taste, smell, touch, see, hear. We communicate with the spirit world with our spirit through what is called intuition or inner promptings.

Therefore, in order to worship and fellowship with God a person must possess God's nature. He is a spirit, John 4:24. Your spirit must be born again or born a new before we can connect with God. How do you become born from above and enter into true worship? We must repent of sins, confess and acknowledge that we are sinners ask His forgiveness and then invite Him into our heart to live forever. Paul gives these steps in Romans 10:9,10,13.

> If thou shall confess with your mouth the Lord Jesus and shall believe in your heart that God hath raised Christ from the dead, thou shall be saved, born from above.

> For with the heart one believeth unto righteousness, and with the mouth confession is made unto salvation.

For whoever calls upon the name of the Lord shall be saved. The word is nigh thee, even in they mouth, and in thy heart that is the word of faith, which we preach.

What does fellowship means?

According to Merrian Webster Dictionary fellowship is the state of sharing mutual interests or activities, companionship or friendship. Father God desire to become our friend and companion in this journey of life. He desire to share what's on His heart with us. The only way this can happen is by spending time in prayer, reading, fasting and meditating upon the Word. We will never come to know true worship nor have true fellowship with God to the point of experiencing His power until we get in this place.

If we say that we have fellowship with Him (the Father) and live in darkness (sin) we lie, and do not tell the truth (1 John 1:6).

We must not live a lifestyle of doing wrong and enter His house on Sunday morning expecting to have fellowship with Him. It will not work. He desire truth in our heart not and outward show of the flesh. Some believers reflected this form of attitude toward worship they party all night Saturday and come Sunday morning they appeared to be in right standing with God, but their lifestyle or character reflect something totally different.

Chapter 3

ATTRIBUTES OF TRUE WORSHIP
IN PROPHETIC INTERCESSION

True worship is an expression of our spirit in direct communion with our Maker, sharing and receiving from Him as well as giving Him homage, honor, and reverence for who He is. When we commune with God, our spirit becomes one with Him, and we are on the same page with God. We are connected. First Corinthians 6:17 says, "He who is joined to the Lord is one Spirit. That gives room for the Holy Spirit. Jesus says, "when the Spirit of truth is come he will guide you into all truth; for he shall not speak of himself but whatsoever he shall hear that shall he speak; and he will show you things to come (John 16:13).

> The man without the Spirit does not accept the things that come
> from the Spirit of God, for they are foolishness to him, and he
> cannot understand them, because they are spiritually discerned
> (1 Cor.2:14) NIV.

True worship will usher one into the presence (glory) of the Lord. It will bring at times brokenness or conviction within one's heart. True worship will prompt us to examine ourselves, revealing the true nature of our heart that we may see ourselves the way we really are, without hiding behind the mask. Isaiah 6:5 gives a perfect example of this woe is me; for I am undone; because I am a man of unclean lip. My eyes have seen the King, the Lord of Hosts.

Isaiah was convicted of his sinful condition and saw himself as an unclean man before a Holy God. His sins were revealed, and he saw himself unworthy to be in the presence of a Holy God. Isaiah became broken and confessed he wasn't in his proper place. So often, we find ourselves in a place we know we should not be in. This can refer to life in general and in worship. True worship will reveal the envy, strife, greediness, hatred, lust, pride, anger, evil desires, malice and a host of other things in our hearts that must be repented of. When we are in the presence of God if there is unrighteousness there I believe the ungodly things are brought to the surface so that we can begin to deal with the issues of our heart. True worship is characterized and developed through a waiting attitude. Waiting is another attribute of worship. We must learn to wait before our Father in prayer, reading the word and listening. True worship is submission of the whole person, spirit, soul and body.

True worship will cause one to examine ourselves, our motives and the way we respond to people and situation. The question was asked in Psalm, Who shall stand in His Holy Place (His presence) he that has clean hands and a pure heart, Psalm. 24:3, 4. From this place you can petition, intercede, declare and do spiritual warfare. This is a place where your prayers can cause change to take place in the earth.

Here are a list of priorities we are commanded to pray about:

Pray for all those in authority including the fivefold ministry gifts (Ephesians 4:11-16; Romans. 10:14, 15).

For Kings/President	1 Timothy 2:1-6; Colossians 4:1-6
For the peace of Jerusalem	Psalms 122:6,7
For the Saints/or body of Christ	Ephesians 6:18
For Sinners/those who do not know Christ	Psalms 2:8

Prompting of prophetic burdens

The burden of prophetic intercession is the result of a growing conviction regarding the purpose of God for our time. God, through the Holy Spirit gently nudge you to pray so He can intervene. When we move and pray in these moments of prompting we bring changes to people lives causing many to escape deadly situations. Daniel had a dream regarding his nation and didn't know what it meant. He was sensitive to the timing and season of God. Daniel sense something was about to happen a change was about to take place and he desired to know what it was. Therefore, he sought God through fasting and prayer. He entered into a time of confession, intercession, repentance and he began to confess the sins of his people as though it was his own. God supernatural sent angels to reveal the interpretation of his dream after fasting for three whole weeks. Daniel interceded for fulfillment of revelation concerning his people (Daniel 9:2 referring to Jeremiah 29:10).

Whether it is preached, prayed, or prophesied, a thing is only prophetic if it brings you into knowledge of what's on the heart and mind of God. What has God placed on your heart for our times? What is that burden you're carrying for the Lord, for our city, for a person, for your nation? Nehemiah's burden was similar to Daniel's.

I beseech thee O Lord God of heaven, the great and awesome God, who preserves the covenant . . . let thine ear now be attentive and thine eyes open to hear the prayer of thy servant which I am praying before thee now, day and night, on behalf of the sons of Israel thy servants, confessing the sins of the sons of Israel which we have sinned against thee; I and my Father's house have sinned (Nehemiah 1:5, 6).

Nehemiah did not ignore the condition of Israel, the tragedy that had stripped her of her land, city, temple and glory. Nevertheless, he found his hope in his knowledge of God, knowing that he is a covenant keeping God. Despite what the church today appears to be, the prophetic intercessor does not base his praying on either good or bad conditions, but rather on the promises and word of God. Prophetic intercession is our conspiring together with God, breathing into situations through prayer in order to bring life. God desires to share His secrets. You share your secrets with the person you trust, who isn't going to say everything they know and God is the same way. Instead of saying it, you pray it, and you pray for mercy in the situation, mercy always triumphs over judgment (James 2:13).

Prophetic acts and demonstrations

A prophetic act of shouting, marching and praise brought down an entire city. This was a divine strategy and plan of God. This same principle can be used today. Not only was this a prophetic act, but also a divine weapon. Psalm 149:6-8 says, "Let the high praises of God be in their mouth, and a two edged sword in their hand, to execute vengeance on the nations and punishments on the peoples; to bind their kings with chains, and their nobles with fetters of iron.

Prophetic acts are literally acting out the prophetic messages God gives. Prophetic acts have two directions: One is toward God and the other is toward the enemy in warfare. Prophetic acts and demonstrations are declarations of God's power and will being manifested. Prophetic acts involve the whole person (body, soul, and spirit). They capture our attention fully. When God instructed Joshua to have the children of Israel march around the city of Jericho seven times this was a prophetic act that was mixed with prophetic praise which in turned cause the Jericho walls to come tumbling down (Josh 6:8, 9).

So the people shouted when the priests blew the trumpets. And it happened when the people heard the sound of the trumpet, and the people shouted with a great shout, that the wall fell down flat. Then the people went up into the city, every man straight before him, and they took the city (Josh 6:20).

Prophetic acts sometimes seem unusual and strange in there appearance but can be powerful in breaking down strongholds or staying the hand of the enemy. We can see an example of a prophetic act with the Prophet Agabus giving Paul instruction as he began to demonstrate what will befall Paul when he goes to Jerusalem. The Prophet Agabus began to take his scarf tie it around Paul to demonstrate how the religious leaders were going to bind him. This prophetic act was fulfilled (Acts 21:10-11).

[10]A certain prophet named Agabus came down from Judea.

[11]When he had come to us he took Paul's belt, bound his own hands and feet, and said, Jews at Jerusalem bind the man who owns this belt and deliver him into the hands of the Gentiles.

[12]And when we heard these things both we and those from that place pleaded with him not to go up to Jerusalem.

Other Prophetic acts

Ezekiel was given instructions to lie on his left side as a prophetic act for the house of Israel for 390 days and on the right side for 40 days a day for each year for Israel's iniquity (Ezekiel 4:1, 2).

Moses lift up his rod over the Red Sea allowing the people to pass over on dry land and the water returned. Moses stretched his hand over the sea and at daybreak the water returned to its usual place (Ex.14:27).

Many times we perform prophetic acts not realizing it. Leroy, my husband was led to perform a prophetic act within a certain area of our city. We place signs with a white flag representing that the territory belonged to Jesus. They were placed on east, west, north and south. At that time we did not realize that this was called a prophetic act, we were just obeying the Holy Spirit.

On another occasion in my prophetic intercession prayer journey, while lying in bed I begin to experience what seem like someone was squeezing my throat I could barely breathe. Immediately my sister came to mind and I began to pray for her while trying to breathe in between. This was a prophetic act or prophetic demonstration of someone being choked. I was literally standing in prayer for her because she was unable to do so herself. I experienced what she was going through. The following morning after arriving at her home, she appeared to be well. I told her the dream and asked if she was okey. She later informed me that someone that same night tried to strangle her. At that time she was in an abusive relationship and God stepped into her situation and I begin to intercede for her life. The enemy strongholds were broken and a way was open for her to be delivered and finally be release from that destructive relationship. That is why it is so important to immediately respond to the Spirit prompting because lives are at stake.

Shifting from intercession to a prophetic mold

Shifting from an intercession prayer mode to a prophetic intercession mode often times begin with a person praying simple prayer petitions then all of a sudden there is a shift in your voice tone. You begin to speak forth with authority as you shifted gears in the realm of the Spirit and the power of the Holy Spirit energizes your prayer. It seem as though words begin to bubble up or pour forth from your inner most being like water into a water fall. You begin to pray prayers beyond their natural knowledge empowered by the Holy Spirit. As we begin to move forward in this vein of pray God will begin to give one more and more revelation of His will, purpose and plan in various situations. Obedience is very key. This is what true intercession is all about, standing in the gap for others that are unable to stand for themselves. It is literally fighting against the forces of evil to stay their hand in the matter.

We dare not leave this session of prophet intercession without speaking on the gift of intercession.

Chapter 4

WHAT IS INTERCESSION?

So I sought for a man among them who would make a wall,
and stand in the gap before me on behalf of the land, that I
should not destroy it; but I found no one.

—Ezekiel 22:30

What is intercession? Intercession is being an advocate on behalf of someone else physically or spiritually. Spiritual intercession is standing in another place before God to stay the hand of destruction. Intercession is a prayer shield to ward off the attacks of the enemy. God said to Ezekiel that he looked for an intercessor that would stand in the gap but found none. Spiritual intercession is the hand of God reaching down and connecting with our problem, situations, circumstance and affairs. Spiritual intercession is a background support ministry to the body of Christ. This is a very important assignment. Much evil and various sins have entered our world because we as intercessors are not faithful in guard duty thereby opening the door to the spirit of destruction. God saw that there was no man/woman and wondered that there was no intercessor, Isaiah 59:16. God said to Ezekiel I looked for someone to stand before Me that I may not destroy the land. If intercessors were on there guard in prayer God would not have any need to say He was unable to find a intercessor. Were are the faithful intercessors? As intercessors we operate and move in two worlds, the physical and spiritual. Therefore, it is imperative to guard your post.

Any effective prophetic intercessor must have a quiet place, a place to get away and be alone. The Psalmist says, "Be still, and know that I am God, Psalms 46:10". On many occasions Jesus went to a solitary place to pray and to be alone, especially right after ministering. Very early in the morning, while it was still dark, Jesus would arise and went to a solitary place, where He prayed, Mark 1:35. Another requirement for effective intercessor is being righteous before God. That mean confess and repent unconfessed sin and clothe yourselves in righteousness. When entering into the presence of God and it seem as though you have difficulty getting into the presence of God, begin by sitting still and begin to speak in your heavenly language for it makes your faith stronger. But you, dear friends, build yourselves up in your most holy faith and pray in the Holy Spirit, Jude 20". Intercessors have a built-in warning system, which operates well in advance of anything being seen. Usually the signs are:

- A sense or feeling in their spirit that something is not quite right. They may not know what is wrong, but they know that something is not right in a particular situation.
- A strong desire to get alone with the Lord.
- A sudden weeping or groaning comes over you
- Then waiting on the Holy Spirit for his guidance as to how and what to pray
- Doing what the Holy Spirit says, pray the burden until the weight lifts off the heart.

The character of an intercessor

What is character? Character is an evaluation of individuals' moral or qualities, which includes behaviors (the way you act) and habits (what you do). Character is the real you. The character of intercessors should be humility, loyalty, integrity, honesty and faithfulness. Intercession should be a lifestyle in every born again believer's life. In the life of an intercessor I believe integrity and humility are the most important.

What Is Intercessory Prayer?

"If they are prophets and have the word of the Lord, let them plead with the Lord Almighty," Jeremiah 27:18.

What is prayer intercession? Prayer intercession is prayer petitions on behalf of others, people, situation and circumstance as well as reminding God of his promises. Plead means to appeal, entreat, solicit, pray, supplicate and petition.

Who are prayer intercessors? A prayer intercessor is someone who continually maintains a prayer guard for the church, its members and other individuals to defend, propel and position it to excel in its assigned region/ territory and endeavors. They are the ones who stand in the gap for others.

Act 22:17-21, gives warning of up coming danger.

[17]Then it happened, when I (Paul) returned to Jerusalem and was praying in the temple that I was in a trance.

[18]And saw Him saying to me, make haste and get out of Jerusalem quickly for they will not receive your testimony concerning me.

[21]Then He said to me; depart, for I will send you far from here to the Gentiles.

Intercessors Responsibilities

You have not gone up to the breaks in the wall to repair it for the house of Israel so that it will stand firm in the battle on the day of the Lord, (Ezekiel 13:5).

1. An intercessor is one who pick up the burden and carry the case before God in behalf of another.

    I have posted watchmen on your walls, O Jerusalem; they will never be silent day or night. You who call on the Lord, give yourselves no rest, and give him no rest till he establishes Jerusalem and makes her the praise of the earth, (Isaiah 62:6-7).

2. A prayer intercessor is one who builds up the hedge or the wall of protection. They builds up the wall in time of battle that could be for a geographical region to keep the enemies out.

    I looked for a man among them who would build up the wall and stand before me in the gap on behalf of the land so I would not have to destroy it, but I found none. So I will pour out my wrath

on them and consume them with my fiery anger, bringing down
on their own heads all they have done, declares the Sovereign
Lord (Ezekiel 22:30-31).

4. A prayer intercessor is one who stands in the gap between God's righteous
   judgment and the need for mercy on people's behalf. The intercessory
   people have a place to stand between God's judgment that is due and yet
   has the need for mercy on the people. They identify with the condition
   of the people and cries for mercy.

A persistence prayer life will condition one for moving into the area of
an intercessor. It is surprising how just a few words can impact our life for
change. Jesus said, "Could you not watch with me one hour," Mat. 26:40.
This statement made by Larry Lee, a television evangelist challenged my
praying time with God from twenty minutes to an hour. As years passed,
God would at time intently awake me at twelve, two and three o' clock to
pray for people and situations. At these times in the morning, the flesh
wishes to cling tightly to the bed.

It will take a while to get accustomed to these hours, when God has called
you to intercession. On one summer, at midnight, I was awaken with a sudden
urge to pray and to intercede for my husband. Immediately the heavenly
language began to flow. I didn't know what was going on; I just obeyed. He
later came home and informed me that three men with a knife tried to take
his life. This is the power of intercession prayer it changed the course of his
life. What the enemy meant for evil, God stepped in and gave him a way
of escape and spared his life. Praise God, he came to know Jesus and is a
minister of his Word today. Ezekiel 22:30 says, Stand in the gap and make
up the hedge. A hedge is a fence, barrier or boundary to keep thing in or out.
That night God through the power of prayer placed a hedge-a supernatural
shield around my husband that the enemy could not take his life.

Being properly aligned

When we speak of alignment we are speaking of the area where you
function best. We must learn to operate within our own position. What
does operate mean? Operate means to work, to perform, to act effectively,
to produce an effect, a place of influence. Therefore, intercessors should be
placed in a position where they will be the most effective. Listed below are
position which intercessor can function this was shared from our intercessor

ministry. These few pointers help identify which function position of an intercessor ministry you might be the most effective.

1. Position One

   • Pray general blessing for people, ministries and events and they come to pass.
   • Build the wall of protection and provision in and around the ones they are praying for.

2. Position Two

   • Have a passion and love for prayer and people. Pray regularly for a specific person or ministry.
   • Receives regular information about the ministry or person, then prays for the needs and see regular results.

3. Position Three

   • This person has a gift of intercession, can pray for long periods-one or more hours daily in prayer. I have two brothers that does this and it have open a great door of revelation to them and others.
   • Loves being in the presence of God.
   • Often time feels or senses the needs of others.
   • Carries the burden and prays until the burden lift.
   • These are armor bearers who stand in front or beside the person or ministry to bring protection and strength.

4. Position Four

   • This type of intercessor is called a prophetic intercessor. This is a special calling or ministry they hear prophetically and pray accordingly. These intercessor see situations from God's point of view.
   • These are watchmen standing on the walls of the city (the church). They have a very close relationship with God and don't hesitate to bring warning at the sight of the enemy.

   Intercessors must be committed to faithfulness honest, have humility and integrity at all times in any level of intercession.

Chapter 5

DISCERNING INTERCESSIONAL NUDGING

Then Jesus came with them to a place called Gethsemane, and said to the disciples, sit here while I go and pray over there.

And He took with Him Peter and the two sons of Zebedee, and He began to be sorrowful and deeply distressed

Then He said to them, My soul is exceedingly sorrowful, even to death. Stay here and watch with me.

—Mat. 26:36-38

Intercession nudging is a spiritual stimulant that alerts our spirit that a situation needs our attention and we should immediately begin to intercede. These intercession nudging can manifest itself in many ways-through watching, weeping, groaning, declaring, supplicating, pleading, shouting, laughing, carrying a burden, through prophetic acts and singing.

These spiritual stimulants gently stir, arouse instant urges in us to pray. It can come in the form of an urgency to pray for someone or any form of the above. Sometime intercessional nudging can come upon you all of a sudden and you may feel sorrowful and begin to weep. It can come as heaviness in your spirit as though you are burden about something but not sure why; just pray. Sometime the nudging comes in the form of a sudden groaning and a desire to speak in your heavenly language you don't know why; just pray. Other time the nudging can be for someone that doesn't know the Lord, you may feel as though you are not saved and the weight of sin is upon your shoulders, just begin to pray for that person's salvation. Pray until you feel a release or a peace in any situation.

An intercessor knows God and has an intimate relationship with Him and knows His heart. This is for every intercessor. Some intercessors are used in birthing or pushing through in prayer the ministries and purposes of the Lord. The intercessor is the one with whom God wants to share His heart. He knows God's heartbeat. An intercessor is a friend of God like Abraham. Abraham believed God, and it was accounted to him for righteousness, James 2:23. When we become God's friend we are placed in a position for God to share His secrets with us. An intercessor can stand in the gap when someone sins, any sin not leading to death can be prayed for James 5:16. The prayer of a righteous man availeth much, 1 John 5:16. One needs to be sensitive to what the Spirit wants to do, if not we can miss it. Intercessor has a specific job of getting equipped with the spirit of mercy. They must have serving capabilities that others do not have. One could say that this intercessor has a shepherd's anointing or quality to his ministry. Because he can see people's hearts, he has to guard his heart from becoming critical. God wants the intercessor to be loving and compassionate. We need God's love as described in 1 Corinthians 13, to be an effective intercessor. The power to love in this way is available to every believer by the Spirit (Romans 5:5).

Our body is the temple of the Holy Spirit and I believe that God appoints intercessors to pray over us when we are going through things ourselves especially, when we are placed in the frontlines, facing the enemy in spiritual warfare, it is good to have intercessors praying for you to stop the flying arrows it is important that certain things be checked at the door and not allowed to enter. Since some intercessors are watchers/doorkeepers, this is one of their assignments to allow or not allow things to enter the earth realm. Intercessors should be able to distinguish what is of the Lord and what is of an evil spirit and begin to pray accordingly. Mark says, Therefore I say to you, Whatever things you desire, when you pray believe that you receive them and you shall have them (Mark 11:24).

When praying, an intercessor will sometimes begin to experience the very pain that is in the body of that person. The intercessor will begin to sigh, groan, wail and to feel the pain of travail and despair. Sometimes it can be very confusing if you are new to intercession because many times you don't understand what's happening. What's happening is the intercessor has actually taken on that person situation in the spirit. You are standing in the gap for that person. You have literally become that person in the spirit, and now as that person, you are petitioning God on there behalf. And the words you are speaking, God is taking hold of them and bring them to pass. This is confirmed in Isaiah 55:11, My word that goes forth out of My mouth; it shall not return to Me empty, but it shall accomplish that which I please, and it shall prosper in the thing for which I sent it.

How does God speak?

> Indeed God speaks once, or twice, yet no one notices it. In a dream, a vision of the night, when sound sleep falls on men, while they slumber in their beds, then He opens the ears of men and seals their instructions (Job 33:14-16).

There are many ways in which God speaks to us. He can speak through his written Word, which is sure. He speaks through signs, wonders, dream, revelation, knowledge and visions. Does God speak through dreams and visions? The answer is yes He does, but most often God speaks to His people through His still small voice, His written words and at times through an audible voice. God spoke through dreams and visions to His prophets in the Old Testament because the priests were the ones to plead for the needs of the people to the Lord and the prophet pleaded the interests of God before the people. The priest was responsible for sending word, and the prophet was responsible for discerning the word and speaking God's burden.

When God reveals something to you about a situation that you know nothing about or gives specific direction for prayer, this is called Prophetic Intercession. It is prayer prayed from the revelation given by God. The Holy Spirit may give you an impression or a word of knowledge regarding people, places, things and situation that you have no earthly information about. Sometime it can be a thought in the mind. He very seldom speaks in an audible voice like our, but I have heard Him speak. It seem as though the voice is coming from a distance or standing above your head atleast with me. Let's look at a few scriptures where other has heard the voice of God.

Hearing the audible voice of God

- Adam and Eve "heard the voice of the LORD God walking in the garden in the cool of the day" (Genesis 8:15).
- Isaiah used this same response when he had his magnificent vision of the Lord in His temple, "Also I heard the voice of the Lord, saying, 'Whom

shall I send, and who will go for us?' Then said I, Here am I; send me (Isaiah 6:8).

- God spoke many times to Moses, most famously from the bush which wouldn't stop burning. There is an intimacy that was developed between God and Moses (Exodus 3:2).
- The LORD would speak to Moses face to face, as a man speaks with his friend (Exodus 33:11).

Hearing the still small voice of God from within our spirit

- For he is our God; and we are the people of his pasture, and the sheep of his hand.

    To day if ye will hear his voice (Psalms 95:7).
- And other sheep I have, which are not of this fold: them also I must bring, and they shall hear my voice; and there shall be one fold, and one shepherd (John 10:16).
- My sheep hear my voice, and I know them, and they follow me (John 10:27).
- As never before, we need to be His Sheep, listening for His voice.
- Behold, I stand at the door, and knock: if any man hear my voice, and open the door, I will come in to him, and will sup with him, and he with me (Revelation 3:20).

    In the older day, God spoke with an audible voice on many occasions, but in our times, He has encouraged believers to listen to the still small voice from within. That is what Elijah did.

    God, said go forth and stand on the mountain before the Lord, and behold, the Lord passed by, and a great and strong wind . . . The Lord was not in the wind and after the wind an earthquake, but the Lord was not in the earthquake; and after the earthquake, a fire, but the Lord was not in the fire: and after the fire a still small voice . . . and suddenly a voice came to him and said, what are you doing here Elijah (1 Kings 19:11-12).

As God passed by Elijah on the mountain Elijah heard a strong wind, an earthquake, and a fire, but God wasn't in any of those things. But after the fire, God spoke with Elijah through a still small voice. God desires to speak with His children the problem is we are too busy too hear Him. God doesn't speak in an audible voice that often to His children because He is trying to get believers to a point of learning how to rely on the inner witness there spirit.

In hearing the voice of God we must develop our listening skills. There are times when you talk and there are time when God talks this is call communication. This is where we begin to develop a personal relationship with the Father. Jesus said in John 10:27, "My sheep hear my voice and I know them and they follow me." We know Him and follow Him through the person of the Holy Spirit. We learn His voice by spending quality time in prayer and learning His ways by studying His Word. When you hear God's voice, you know that it's Him because of what He says, which will always be in agreement with his written Word. Paul said, there are many kind of voices in the world . . . we must test them to see if they are of God, 1 Cor. 14:10. How? By the Word. If a voice tells you to do anything contrary or doesn't agree with God's Word, rest assure it's not God. When hearing the voice of God it's a gentle guide, encourages and gives hope. His voice can at time be authoritative when He is trying to get a point over to you, Isa. 40:11; James 3:17). God leads, Satan drives (John 10:4-10). God convicts, Satan condemns and brings guilt (John 16:8-11).

Chapter 6

WHAT DOES IT MEANS TO BE A PROPHET?

And He said, hear now my words: If there be a prophet among you, I the Lord will make myself known unto him in a vision, and will speak to him in a dream. My servant Moses is not so, who is faithful in all mine house. With him I will speak mouth to mouth (Number 12:6-8).

Surely the Lord God will do nothing, but he revealeth his secret unto his servants the prophets (Amos 3:7).

A prophet is a divine messenger of God who hears His voice and speak forth what he/she hear from the mind of God. He/she is a servant of God. We can't place all prophets in the same bag. They are not the same; each one carries a different gifting anointing. We will speak more on this is chapter nine. The Prophet has the authority to bind and loose, to open and to shut. A good example of this was the Prophet Ezekiel, he prayed that it would not rain for three and half years and it didn't. After the three and half years expired he again prayed that the rain would come, and it did. Elijah was a man just like us. He prayed earnestly that it would not rain, and it did not rain on the land for three and a half years. Again he prayed, and the heavens gave rain, James 5:17, 18. The prophet has the ability to shut up the heaven and open it. The prophet has been given authority to issue a decree to open and shut things up, to open and close spirituals portals. An intercessor who have a prophetic anointing I believe have this dimension of authority.

The Lord lays out a few principles, whereby we might know when He has set a prophet in office.

- It is the Lord who set a person in an office; it has nothing to do with one's own ability, Eph. 4:11-13. The purpose for setting one in the office is to equip the Saints for the work of the ministry and to build up the body of Christ.
- He will reveal Himself in a vision or dream. If there be a prophet the Lord will make Himself known unto Him in a vision. And he said, Hear now my words: If there be a prophet among you, I the LORD will make myself known unto him in a vision, and will speak unto him in a dream (Numbers 12:6).
- He will operate in the gift of revelation.
- He will not give his own interpretation, but God. "Knowing this first, that no prophecy of the scripture is of any private interpretation (2 Pet. 1:20).
- His overall goal is to edify the body not self. But he that prophesieth speaketh unto men to edification, and exhortation, and comfort. He that speaketh in an unknown tongue edifieth himself; but he that prophesieth edifieth the church (1 Corinthians 14:3-4).
- He must believe in the resurrection of Christ. "Every spirit that confesseth that Jesus Christ is come in the flesh is of God: And every spirit that confesseth not that Jesus Christ is come in the flesh is not of God: and this is that spirit of antichrist, whereof ye have heard that it should come; and even now already is it in the world (1 John 4:2-3).
- He is known by his fruit (His character). Ye shall know them by their fruits. Do men gather grapes of thorns, or figs of thistles? Even so every good tree bringeth forth good fruit; but a corrupt tree bringeth forth evil fruit. A good tree cannot bring forth evil fruit, neither can a corrupt tree bring forth good fruit (Matthew. 7:16-18).

Prophet credentials

> For who hath stood in the counsel of the Lord, and hath perceived and heard his word? Who hath marked his word and heard it. (Jeremiah 23:18).

According the Roget's Super Thesaurus, credentials is being able to produce some form of reference, paper documentation, testimonial, license, letter of reference attesting the qualification/character of an individual. It has to do with a person's credibility, his trustworthiness and integrity. First they must be a person who have stood in the counsel of God, has an ear to hear the voice of God and take heed to the Word of God. How can one know a prophet or receive a prophet in God's name? One should be able to recognize the principles set forth by God from the person's testimony. The Bible says, you should know them by their fruits (works, action and words). When looking for a true prophet, look for the following:

- His experience will be initiated by God.
- God will reveal Himself in a vision.
- God will speak in a dream or a conversation.
- The person's life should cast a shadow with these things in it.
- A prophet of God will always be trying to bring people to God (repentance from wrong ways) and not be turning or releasing them to the pleasures of their own life. He will not only be saying that "God is" but also that Jesus is.
- He will always bring attention to God and not himself.
- He will be a person on a mission, big or small.
- A prophet will speak from something he has seen, in a vision or in a vision in his spirit. It will not be his imagination, but rather it will be something given at the will of the Holy Spirit.

Prophets Functions

Every prophet or prophetess should operate through the avenue of love. Paul says you can do all the things and not have love it is no good. Love is long suffering, its kind, its not jealous, it does not boast or inflated itself, not selfish, does not rejoice over the wrong of others, but rejoices in the truth. If a prophet does not display these qualities of love be on guard. The Apostle Paul said,

Though I speak with the tongues of men and of angels, but have not love, I have become as sounding brass or a clanging cymbal. And though I have the gift of prophecy and understand all mysteries and all knowledge, and though I have all faith, so that I could remove mountains, but have not love, I am nothing. And though I bestow all my goods to feed the poor, and though I give my body to be burned, but have not love, it profits me nothing (1 Cor.13:1-13).

Function defines assignment or duties. Function defines the duty or action for which a person is particularly fitted or employed. According to the Merriam Webster Dictionary, function is a professional or official position. As a prophet you have a professional position in the house of God. You are now employed by God, given a specific job assignment or duties to perform for His Kingdom. Therefore, the functions/purposes of the prophetic office is to prophecy, bring edification, exhortation and comfort and also to bring correction, warning, direction and judgment, 1 Corinthians 14:3-4. The prophet's main function is to be a bridge between man and God.

The prophet is to receive the word from the Lord and communicate it in a way that will edify that person or minister. He or she is God's mouth piece. The seasonal prophet not only plows up the weeds of sin but replants with good seed (words that edify and build up). God gave Jeremiah an official position. Behold, I have put my words in your mouth. See, I have this day set you over the nations and over the kingdoms, to root out and to pull down, to destroy and to throw down, to build and to plant (Jeremiah 1:9-10).

The prophet whose purpose is to correct should not only be able to tell you what's wrong, but he should also be able to tell you how to correct the problem. That means the prophet has to stand in God in his counsel, which is the key element required to make sound judgments and to be successful. As a prophet, the more you stand in God's counseling, the more you learn of God's ways and thoughts. You are then better able to make sound judgments based on God's will, not man's will. Judge not according to the appearance, but judge righteous judgment (John 7:24).

The prophet purpose also includes perfecting the saints for the work of ministry, edifying, building up and teaching the Body of Christ to become mature in the faith.

And he gave some, apostles; and some, prophets; and some, evangelists; and some, pastors and teachers; for the perfecting of the saints, for the work of the ministry, for the edifying of the body of Christ: Till we all come in the unity of the faith, and of the knowledge of the Son of God, unto a perfect man, unto the measure of the stature of the fullness of Christ (Ephesians 4:11-13).

1. A Prophet is a person set apart (man or women) whose only concern is being accountable to the Lord. When a prophet speaks he or she should not expect to receive self glory or self praise for their words. They're Jesus words.

2. A prophet has the ability to bring the anointing presence of God into a meeting that will change the atmosphere. Why? Because a prophet has the ability to move into the throne room very quickly. And when you move into the throne room you begin to communicate what heaven would like to release from the throne room of God while your spirit is in the presence of God. Then you begin to communicate outward into the very place were you are.

3. Some Prophets will speak as the hammer of God which comes to break in pieces the lies and deceptions of the false doctrines presently being taught and to bring deliverance from bondage (Jeremiah 23:28, 29).

Chapter 7

RECOGNIZING THE DEMEANOR
OF A MILITANT PROPHET

When we think of a person who is militant the first thing that comes to mind is confronational, fighting or combat. A Militant prophet is an individual or a group of individual engaged in aggressive physical or verbal combat for a cause. They are the true soldiers who do not mind being on the front line. Their demeanor is that of a soldier who is ready to defend his faith and belief. The Apostle Paul has this kind of attitude and was willing to die for it. Demeanor is the way we carry ourselves, your conduct. Demeanor consists of (behavioral attributes), the way a person behaves toward other people. A Militant prophet must be very careful of their demeanor because they can come off as hard and uncaring. Militaristic is a military term used in war. Militaristic is defined as the belief or desire of a government and it's people that a country should maintain a strong military capability and be prepared to use those militaristic forces to defend or promote national interests of that country.

Basically, this is saying a country has a right to defend itself against its enemies. As citizens of the Kingdom of Heaven, believers/intercessors has a right to defend the Kingdom of God against its enemies. Elijah was a militant prophet, and we can see this quality in him when he challenges Ahab and the prophets of Baal, 1 King 18:19-40. The militant prophet hates the devil with a passion and will not tolerate his tricks. This class of prophets doesn't care one way or the other if you agree or don't agree with them as long as they know God said it; that's all that matters. A militant prophet seems to have a bull dog attitude; they will not relent until they have captured or destroyed their prey. I am reminded of my father when God saved him.

God said to Dad tell My people the wages of sin is death, but the gift of God is eternal life, Romans. 6:23. He then said, a good hunting dog catches his prey first and lick his wounds later. In other words, we must have that dogmatic attitude that for God, I live or die trying. The militant prophet has the grace and anointing to flow strong in spiritual warfare because of their militant disposition.

The first time I saw the word militaristic was when I read Dr. Paula A. Price's newly released book entitled, The Prophets Handbook: A guide to prophecy and its operation. It seem as though after all these years I could identify myself, my husband, my mother and understand why they act the way they did. According to Dr. Price, Prophets Handbook, the militaristic prophet emphasizes the raging, ongoing battles with the forces of darkness. They have keen insight into the strategies and tactics of Satan and innately understand how to deal with them. This class of prophets carries a governing anointing to defend, bring order and to promote spiritual interests of the Kingdom of God. Have you ever thought of yourself being in God's military army this position shouldn't be taken lightly. We're co-labourours with God. My mother is another militant person of whom I have gained insight.

Ora Stokes, my mother is a prophetess that has a militant or militaristic anointing. This anointing has no tolerance for sin and will fight when ever confronted with it. She has a keen insight about the strategies and tactics of Satan and is not easily fooled by people nor their intentions, because of this anointing she is not very well received by people. She is a no non sense person and has very low tolerance for foolishness. She is very sensitive to spiritual things and has the boldness to speak what is revealed. God also deals with her as a dreamer who is very accurate when it comes to things in the spirit realm. She often time can recognize motive of people working behind the scene even before it has been revealed in the natural. She is a woman of great wisdom, spiritual insight sound judgment.

Understanding Military Tactics

Military tactics (Greek: *taktikē*, the art of organizing an army) are the techniques for using weapons or military units in combination for engaging and defeating an enemy in battle. Notice what the definition states. First, military tactics is the art of organizing. It is an organized unit or group. Second, it has the ability and know what techniques and weaponry to use in battle. Third, military tactics is knowing how to engage the enemy in order to defeat him.

The key point is that everyone should flow as a unit or group with the same focus the same target in a corporate setting. How does it look for the captain of a group of soldiers to be on a battlefield, with each soldier doing their own thing. Not very good and plus it shows disunity within the group. We are so accustomed to grouping all intercessors in one group and very seldom brainstorm with each other to see what's on our heart/mind that it may be released to the body of Christ. Intercessors should meet as a corporate group and discuss various prayer techniques, ways and various prayer weapons that might work good together to defeat our spiritual enemy. We don't think of the body of Christ militarily, but I believe we should at times. Everyone has their function; it's just many time we don't know our function and we miss it.

Prayer strategies: The Night Watch

> Listed below is the example of a prayer strategic God gave for my city. This was given by revelation of God's Spirit. The mandate is: Divide your city into four sections, North side, South side, East side and West side. It doesn't matter where you are. Then each church and individuals located on their side of town will be responsible for a prayer watch and a time to pray. These intercessors are call to watch over the cities and pray. They are on a Divine assignment.

Night Watch

- Churches and individuals living on the North side of your town pray from 6 a.m-9 a.m.
- Churches and individuals living on the South side of your town pray from 12 midnight-3 a.m.
- Churches and individuals living on the East side of your town pray from 9 a.m-12:00 midnight.
- Churches and individuals living on the West side of your town pray from 3 a.m-6 a.m.

What are some Military strategies for prophetic intercesion

Military strategy is a national defense policy implemented by military organizations to pursue desired strategic goals. Derived from the Greek strategos, strategy is "the art of arrangement" of troops. Military strategy deals with the planning and conduct of campaigns, the movement, disposition of forces, and the deception of the enemy.

Intercessors should have strategic goals or plans when praying. We should ask the why are we praying for this situation, what do we expect to come from praying this way, who do we approach it and so forth. We need intercessors that are able to in the spirit disposition the forces of the enemy, to warn of the enemy's plans and strategies.

What is military logistics? Military logistics is the planning and carrying out the movement and maintenance of any military forces.

Military operations and aspects are:

- Design, development, distribution, maintenance, evacuation and disposition. Intercessors should be able to design and develop successful warfare strategy and know when to pull out of a place or stop one assignment and move to another. This is called knowing how to disposition oneself.
- Being able to Move between earth and heaven.

This is the purpose of the military logistics unit to prepare for those who are wounded, hurt, hospitalized (church or the marketplace) and to get them to a safe place. Some time this means praying with them, encouraging or just offering a listening ear. We need a unit of intercessor who is able to minister to the wounded and hurt. Intercessors should be able to design strategy, to defend the enemy and still be able to keep on course in the spirit. We are not there yet, but I believe it's coming to pass.

Battle space

Battle space in this book is another name for battle ground. Battle space is where the battle will be won or lost. It is a centralize location. The battle we are speaking of begins here in our mind. This is another military term little is known about. When we look at the word battle, it means a combat between two or more parties. The first battle we must confront is the war or battle going on within our own mind. Battle are being waging every day, either spiritually, emotionally, physically and psychologically.

Battle space is a unified strategy to integrate and combine armed forces for the military theater of operations, including air, information, land, sea and space. It includes the environment, factors, and conditions that must be understood to successfully apply combat power, protect the force or complete the mission. From the definition we learn that we should be prepared for battle in any condition, rain or snow, good or bad nothing should keep one from fulfilling one's assignment or mission. This includes enemy and friendly armed forces, weather, terrain, and the electromagnetic spectrum within the operational areas and areas of interest. In other words, you must count up the cost. We should ask ourselves is this battle worth fighting or should I choose another time. We should ask ourselves what will be the outcome, what weapon should I use. All these factors should be considered before waging an all-out war. The important thing we should notice about the battle space:

- It includes strategy for the air, land, sea and space.
- It takes into account what's going on in and around the battlefield, which includes the environment, weather condition: warm, sunny, rain, snow, ice as well as the territory: mountain, field, slopes, hills etc.

All conditions must be understood to successfully apply combat power, protect the force and complete the mission in any battle. When in a battle we must observe our surrounding, what's going on, what's being said, what is the situation, should I make a move, leave it alone or should I call for back up. Many people try to fight their battle alone and sometime lose the battle. This is stated in Proverb 11:14, when there is no helping suggestion the people will have a fall, but with a number of wise guides they will be safe. (BBE).

Weapons of Warfare

> For the weapon of our warfare is not carnal, but mighty to God to the pulling down of stronghold, casting down arguments and every high thing that exalts itself against the knowledge of God, bringing every though into captivity to the obedience of Christ. And being ready to punish all disobedience when your obedience is fulfilled (1I Cor. 10:4-5).

A weapon is a tool used either in hunting, attacking, or defending in combat for the purpose of stopping the enemy or destroying the enemy weapons, equipment, and defensive structures through application of force in the natural. Weapons can be used to threaten direct or indirect contact. Weapons can be as simple as the use of a stick or as complex as the use of a missile. Anything capable of being used to damage, incapacitate, destroy can be referred to as a weapon even psychologically, such as mind game. As believers we neglect to think about the fact that the enemy of our soul doesn't war fairly. He uses I believe psychologically weapons on us more than any other. This is the reason why we need the armor of God.

- Every Christian is commanded to "put on the armor" before going into warfare.
  Why an armor? Because you are a soldier. Why armor? Because you are in a battle. A spiritual war is going on, God says, "put on the whole armour of God that ye may be able to stand against the wiles of the devil (Ephesians 6:11).
- For we wrestle not against flesh and blood, but against principalities, against powers, against the rulers of the darkness of this world, against spiritual wickedness in high places." This is not a battle against people, but we are in a warfare against supernatural forces evil (Ephesians 6:12).
- The Word of God says, Finally, my brethren be strong in the Lord, and in the power of his might. It is in his might, not our strength. Again it says, Not by might, nor by power, but by my spirit, saith the Lord of hosts (Zech. 4:6).
- They (believers) overcame him (Satan) by the blood of the Lamb and by the word of their testimony (Revelation 12:11).
- The apostle Paul instructed Timothy to "endure hardness, as a good soldier of Jesus Christ (II Tim. 2:3).

Singing and praising are divine strategies

> And when they began to sing and to praise, the Lord set ambushments against the children of Ammon, Moab, and mount Seir, which came against Judah; and they were smitten (II Chronicles 20:22).

[15] And he said, Hearken ye, all Judah, and ye inhabitants of Jerusalem, and thou king Jehoshaphat, thus saith the Lord unto you, be not afraid nor dismayed by reason of this great multitude; for the battle is not yours, but God'.

[16] Tomorrow go ye down against them: behold, they come up by the cliff of Ziz; and ye shall find them at the end of the brook, before the wilderness of Jeruel.

[17] Ye shall not need to fight in this battle : set yourselves, stand ye still, and see the salvation of the Lord with you, O Judah and Jerusalem: fear not, nor be dismayed; tomorrow go out against them: for the Lord will be with you.

[21] And when he had consulted with the people, he appointed singers unto the Lord, and that should praise the beauty of holiness, as they went out before the army, and to say, Praise the Lord; for his mercy endureth for ever.

Chapter 8

WHO ARE CONFRONTATIONAL PROPHETS?

The confrontational prophets is similar to the militant prophets. They don't mind facing the enemy head on. Again we see Elijah who was a confrontational prophet. He challenges the false prophet of Jezebel to a showdown. (11 King 18:1-39).

Confrontation is the act of confronting, a face-to-face meeting the clashing of forces or ideas, conflict involving armed forces, discord or a clash of opinions and ideas. This type of prophets is not afraid of people faces. They display "Holy boldness," it doesn't matter who you are if they have a word from God for you it will be delivered. They see only black or white, right or wrong and no in between. They are very keen on detecting heresy in the body of Christ and those around them. It can be in the form of sin, erroneous teaching or a ungodly lifestyle. They are very firm about defending the faith and protecting the Body of Christ.

My husband, Leroy is a confrontational prophet who also flows strong in a militaristic apostolic anointing. He has always had ongoing battles with the forces of darkness. Some nights he would awaken and tell of his encounters with the spirits of darkness, describing how they looked and how they smelt. He too is very keen in the spirit and can recognize the strategies and tactics of Satan. He often tells me things about what the church body should be doing and how to go about it. We have had many disagreement regarding church issues I tell him to address his concerns to the ones that are able to make the changes. He is a prophet with a breakthrough anointing, strong spiritual discernment, wisdom and powerful in the spirit world. What do I mean about transferring anointing is when he has the gift of healing operating on him and he touches or prays for you that anointing sometime release upon you and you find yourself doing healing as he does.

With his confrontational anointing as a prophet he seems to be always on the attack, with an axe like word. He has a harsh edge to his messages which cause many people to not want to be around him. His words carry strong rebuke and chastening to those him meet. I also suggest that he soften the way he response to people. His message carries with it warning of impending judgment which I have seen come to pass. I have seen this happen on a few occasions and reminded him to be careful on how and what he say. He constantly speaks about sin and repentance. Not only is he a militaristic, confrontational prophet, but also carries a strong evangelistic anointing. Every day he go out loading with tracts to distribute because he says souls are being snatched into hell constantly while we, as Saints of God sit behind titles and the four walls doing nothing but religious programs.

How I came to operate in the prophetic realm, first I believe you can't be made a prophet or prophetess. Your DNA makeup determine who you are. It is passed down from your family line or on special occasions as God sometime does. I believe you must be born with your God given gift, even though it takes some time to develop it. My mom is a prophetess and my Father, Eugene Stokes was evangelist and I have inherited spiritual tactics from both my mother the prophetess, and my father the evangelist. For God uses me in strong motivational preaching, teaching, revelation, word of wisdom, dreams, the spiritual warfare, and intercession. I didn't accept my calling as a prophetess until years later in my ministry even though I was already operating in it. My advice to any one who may think you are a prophet or prophetess, receive your confirmation from God and not man. Therefore, you will not have to wrestle with it later.

Militaristic prophetic traits

- They have keen spiritual insight in to the strategies and tactics of Satan and know how to deal with them.
- They have low tolerance for mingling with sin.
- Doesn't compromise with sin tell it like it is, cut no corners.
- They have power in the realm of the spirit, what they say happens quickly.

Confrontational prophetic traits

- They always seem to be on the attack with strong rebuke and chasten word.
- Always speak of God's judgment
- They seem to never have anything kind to say. This kind of prophet can be very judgmental and need to practice on their message delivery, love and mercy because their word has power to plant, build, uproot, reveal and judge.

All prophets carries a different mantle anointing. We have grouped all prophets as being the same as we did all prayers because before knowledge was increase, we didn't know the different. The Lord revealed this truth to me a few years ago. And up to this time I have never seen it in a book or heard of it. Prophets can carry various anointing and functions.

Chapter 9

PROPHET CALLING AND ELECTION

Therefore, brethren, be even more diligent to make your
calling and election sure, for if you do these things you will
never stumble.

—1 Peter 1:10

What does it means to be called? In this case a calling or to be called is a Divine summon from God regarding a spiritual vocation or profession for the Kingdom. It is a strong inner urge or prompting or conviction of an inner summoning. The prophet calling is a Divine invitation to become a partner with God in helping fulfill His plans and purpose on earth. The word call is the Greek word metakaleo, which imply change. Calling means "to be called or summon from one place to another." The prophet now has the ability to operate between two worlds, heaven and earth. It is a Divine office, ministry or/and calling/summon from God set in the Body of Christ for the perfecting of the saints, for the work of the ministry, for the edifying of the body of Christ, Eph. 4:12. Looking at the word election will give a better understanding of our calling. According to Dictionary. com, election means "the selection of a person or persons for office." By placing you into this office God has given you the right and ability to make choices according to this office as long as its in agreement with His word. Prophets have a great responsibility and are selected by God to operate in this unique office.

As stated earlier prophets are the mouthpieces of God hearing what he says in the heaven and releasing it back into the earth. They are God representatives.

All prophets are not seers but all seers are prophets each carries a different anointing as we will see below. A seer is a prophet with a strong vision anointing. He is a prophet that's able to peer in to the spirit realm and declares that which cannot be known by natural means and prophesy what he sees in the physical realm. According to Vine's Expository Dictionary of Old and New Testament Words, the Hebrew term for seer is ra'eh meaning to see, 1 Sam. 9: 9. It is also translate as the word nabhi, meaning one in whom the message from God springs forth or to whom anything is secretly communicated. The prophet is one upon whom the Spirit of the Lord rested (Number 11:17-20).

According to Vine's Expository Dictionary of Old and New Testament the word, prophesy is "propheteis" meaning to speak forth the mind and counsel of God, "Pro" means forth, "phemi" means to speak. Prophet has the Divine ability to speak forth what they hear from God.

Every prophet is not ordained to go to the nations. If you remain faithful wherever you are in due season God will elevate you, but if not be a good steward. There are many job opening in God's Kingdom. God need prophet in every area of life. He need marketplace prophets to minister to the housewife, in the store, in the streets, in the banks and other areas.

There are so many gifting in the Word, it would boggle the mind to list them all. Listed below are what I call a twofold anointing office. In this section our focus in on the prophet that can flow in their office as well as in another. You will see that a prophet can also have an apostolic anointing, evangelist, pastor and a number of other. In the word of God, "gifts" are stated plainly.

Knowing your prophetic gift

1 Corinthians 12:1, 4-10

- Prophet-Apostolic is a prophet with a keen divine insight and a strong desire to see churches established, not so much in physical location but in the heart of men too. (Eph 4: 11).
- Prophet-Prophet is a prophet with a strong prophet anointing.
- Prophet-Evangelist is a prophet with a strong soul outreach anointing.

- Prophet-Pastor is a prophet with a shepherd/nurturing anointing.
- Prophet-Teacher is a prophet with a strong teaching anointing couple with deep revelation insight.
- Prophet-Psalmist/ worshipers is a prophet with a strong singing anointing. Often time this anointing kick in or is stimuli when they begin to sing or hear music.
- Prophet-Healers is a prophet with a strong healing/miracle anointing.
- Prophet-Deliverer is a prophet with a strong delivering anointing.
- Prophet-Intercessor/ watchman is a prophet with a strong prophetic intercessional anointing to pray, guard, patrol protect an assigned area.
- Prophet-Counselor is a prophet with a strong advisory anointing (Is. 11:2). Nathan gave counsel to David (2 Sam 7:3; 1 King 1:24).
- Prophet-Seer is a prophet with a strong discerning/vision anointing, may also be a dreamer and visionary. They can literally see things in the Spirit (1 Sam. 9:9).
- Prophet-Dancer is a prophet with a strong anointing dance and praise before God. When dance is seductive it is displaying the spirit of Herodias which danced before the king and later asked for the head of John. This form of dancing will causes one to give up their most precious good in spite of the consequences. And to cause weak men to stumble and lose their head as John the Baptist, Mark 6:18-19, because they will no longer be thinking with their head but their heart or feeling.
- Prophetic-Writer is prophet with a strong ability to communicate the message of God to make it understandable through the media of writing. Habakkuk and the Apostle John were prophets that had the ability to write there prophecy.

I also believe prophets can operate in one or more of the nine gifts of the spirit, and these gifts can be used interchangeable. For example prophets who operate strong in deliverance also has a strong anointing in the word of wisdom, word of knowledge, and discerning of spirit and so on. As concerning the fivefold ministry apostle, prophet, evangelist, pastor, and teacher the same applies to them. We have touched on the prophet anointing combined with the nine gifts. Even though the apostle office the same can apply. It is believed that apostles can flow in all office, but I am convinced that every person has a dominate gift in which they operate stronger in and other gifts to enhance it.

Office of the Apostle

- All Apostles are not the same, all prophets are not the same, all evangelists are not the same, and all teachers are not the same.
- An Apostle can hold the office of an apostle and can flow strong in the evangelistic, pastor and teacher anointing.

Office of the Pastor

- The office of the pastor has been most demonstrated of this fact. Within your local church you have observed pastors who have a teaching anointing; they want to stay in the word give instructions and imparting knowledge to the people of God.
- Pastors with an evangelistic anointing is always speaking of saving souls, getting people to accept Christ into there life.
- Yet there are other pastors who has a prophetic anointing and flows strong in revelation knowledge and speaking prophetically in there messages.
- A pastor with a healing anointing see to the sick being healed and made whole.
- Pastor with a worshiping anointing sing and offer praise and worship more than they preach the word because this is the vein they best flow in.
- Pastor with a counseling anointing flows strong in word of wisdom and word of knowledge.

The list can go on and on. We process a wealth of gifts and talents in the body of Christ. Let's not box God in He is so huge we can never figure Him out. Just for the record, these gifts are not limited to the fivefold office. But God has regular believers who are sitting on the pew with various gifts just waiting to be released. Because you're not apart of the fivefold ministry doesn't mean you are not gifted, because you are. Each of God's creatures are unique and very gifted. Ask God to show you your gifts.

Prophetic gifting

Paul speaks of many gifts in 1 Corinthians 12:1, 4, 10 and state the primary reason for their function is that we not be unlearned about their operations. These gifts help awaken and activate the Saints for God's purpose, their season and times. Prepare the way for a visitation of God to sound the alarm in times of judgment, transition, and warfare and to bring direction and structural adjustments to body of Christ and movements.

> [1]Now concerning spiritual gifts, brethren I do not want you to be ignorant.

> [4]Now there are diversities of gifts, but the same Spirit.

> [5]There are differences of ministries, but the same Lord.

> [6]And there are diversities of activities, but it is the same God who works all in all.

> [7]But the manifestation of the Spirit is given to each one for the profit of all.

> [8]for to one is given the word of wisdom through the Spirit, to another the word of knowledge through the same Spirit.

> [9]to another faith by the same Spirit, to another gifts of healings by the same Spirit.

> [10]to another the working of miracles, to another prophecy, to another discerning of spirits, to another different kinds of tongues, to another the interpretation of tongues.

> [11]But one and the same Spirit works all these things, distributing to each one individually as He wills.

The prophetic gifting can flow in any number of combinations. For example, a prophet can flow strong in the gift of the word of wisdom and/or word of knowledge and discerning of spirits or one can flow strong in gift of faith, gifts of healings and working of miracles or one can flow strong in various kinds of tongues and interpretation of tongues. There are some that flows strong in prophecy and the word of knowledge. But all work by the same Holy Spirit. God has placed so many gifting and anointing in people, but we have a tendency to focus on a few having people believe that there are only a chosen few who possess the gifts of God. And by doing this, we often time overlook the many gifts within and around the Body of Christ.

We can't box God in and try to specify a small number of gifts and think that's it, because it's not.

Defining the nine gifts

- Word of wisdom—The Divine ability to understand what is revealed.
- Word of knowledge—The Divine ability to know something about a person, place, or thing which is not known by the natural means.
- Faith—Believing God regardless of how it look outwardly.
- Gifts of healings—A Divine gift to bring healing and restoration.
- Working of miracles—A Supernatural acts of God.
- Prophecy—The Divine ability to receive from God the hidden truth and relay it in the natural realm.
- Discerning of spirits—The Divine ability to see or peer into the spirit realm, discerning both angels, demon forces and the Lord Jesus Christ.
- Various kinds of tongues—The Divine ability to speak in a supernatural language that have never been learned, given by the unction of the Holy Spirit.
- Interpretation of tongues—The divine ability to interpret the supernatural message of one who speaks in tongues given by the Holy Spirit.

How to flow in the word of Prophecy

What is prophecy? Prophecy is God's way of speaking to believers about what's on His mind and revealing His hand in the matter.

Prophecy is a word given of what will be before it happens/manifest in the natural. As one writer says, it is the mind of God migrating to the mind of man. It is God getting involved with the affairs of man. Prophecy is God's thoughts revealed or transmitted through the mind of man regarding His plans, purposes, actions and will. The Hebrew word for prophecy means to flow forth, to bubble forth like a fountain to tumble forth to spring forth, to let drop, to lift up. Every believer is encouraged to prophesy, but all are not prophets because they prophesy.

The simple gift of prophecy is to edifying, to strengthen, to build up; exhortation (to encourage) and comfort (to make happy or cheer up), 1 Corinthians 14:3-4.

Prophecy can be revealed through Scriptures which can speak prophetically to the messenger during study times, visions, prayer, dreams and audible voice of which we must be careful and test it by the word of

God. Prophecy can be manifested through inspired utterance of the spirit, foretelling, teaching, writing, singing, also through a word of wisdom, a word of knowledge and discerning into the spirit realm. Prophecy can be past, present and future. A prophet can reveal something regarding your past informing you of detail events that happen to you or it can be a combination of past, present and future. Prophet must be mindful on the proper time and season when to release a prophetic word especially to individuals.

The flow of prophesy

According to Jill Goll's book, "The Seer" the word prophesy is called nabiy, meaning to flow, means to flow forth, bubbling forth like a fountain, to let drop, to lift up, to tumble forth and to spring forth." Nabiy also means to hear and speak and to declare what one has heard. To prophesy in Greek is the word "naba" (naw-bee). I believe that I am a nabiy prophet. When prophesying the words would tumble from my lips like a fountain of water turned on, and there is no stopping it. Seeing this confirms even the more my calling in ministry. The nabiy prophet leans more toward the being audible and verbal. It is more of a communicative inspirational anointing.

When God speaks to you in an audible voice it sound like an actual person speaking but from a distance. Once I attended a service, the praise was very high everyone were praising and magnifying God. There was a certain lady in the back of the church praising and dancing. I thought to myself she is really magnifying God. Then from behind my head came a voice from heaven, Matt. 3:17, the Lord said, she is not sincere her praise is not real. My head did a double take, I looked again and He said, She is faking. God will allow you to see past the smoke screen of a person face, smile and outward appearance and will allow you to see the real motive of their heart. God said to the Prophet Samuel . . . God does not see as humans sees. Humans look at the outward appearance, but the Lord looks into the heart. 1 Samuel 16:7. What is God teaching here: One do not be impress about how people looks on the outside it may or may not be real.

On another occasion, my great mother-in-law had a stroke I was praying for her healing. I cried out to God with all my might and finally He spoke and said, be quiet, she is healed. I continued to pray and cry, then I heard His voice, it came with such powerful authority, saying, "shut up, she is alright." Of cause, I immediately stopped, dried my tears and sniff like a little child after spanking. God is teaching His children to have faith in what He says and to know His voice. Jesus said, "My sheep hear my voice, and I know them, and they follow me" John 10:27. Why is it that so many are being led astray, because they do not know the Lord's voice nor His Word. We must exercise care in the voices we hear and place them side by side with the word of God. If it goes against the Word, please do not listen to it.

Church Prophets or nabiy prophets often work good with leadership. They minister through laying on of hands, relating prophecy to individuals as it is revealed to them. It often utilizes the spiritual gifts of tongues and the interpretation of tongues, prophecy and words of knowledge. This prophet hears a word in their spirit and begins to release this unction of the Holy Spirit. This kind of prophecy is spontaneous operate with a faster flow of release. On the other hand the prophet/seers leans more toward a single-person ministry. The seer anointing emphasizes visions and the revelatory gifts mingled with the gift of discerning of spirits. His flow of delivery is much slower because he explaining what he's seeing. The word prophesy means to speak for another. God called Jeremiah to be His mouthpiece.

> Before I formed you in the womb I knew you, and before you were born I consecrated you; I have appointed you a prophet "nabiy" to the nations (Jer. 1:5).

Prophetic release with the aid of music

What ignites your prophetic flow? I have notice that certain type of music can stir ones anointing to maximize the prophetic flow. Music and singing can be an excellent tool for releasing the prophetic word of the Lord and His power. You might begin by speaking in your heavenly language even though you don't understand, it's creating a harmony in spirit, soul and body, which releases the anointing power of God. Music has the ability to take Your mind, emotions and will and bring them to flow together at the same time creating unity. And your whole spirit soul and body begin to vibrate with the very power of God. And His glory begins to come upon you and begins to shine forth from you as you begin to move into that realm.

Chapter 10

EXPLORING THE OFFICE OF
THE GATEKEEPERS

King David was the one who put the gatekeepers in their places
and their calling was officially confirmed by Samuel the seer
and King David.

—1 Chronicles 9:22

Chief gatekeepers were Shallum, Akkub, Talmon, Ahiman and their brethren.
Shallum of the Korahites and his relatives were responsible for guarding the
tent thresholds, 1 Chron. 9:17-19. Shallum was the firstborn. He had the
responsibility of the bakery and some of his other relatives were responsible
for the showbread. Shallum and his brothers continued the ministry of their
fathers who was a keeper of the entrance to the Lord's camp.

As gatekeepers their job was to kept watch over what came in and what
went out in the tent of meeting. They kept charge of the articles used in
the temple service and the furnishings of the sanctuary, 1 Chron. 9:27-29.
Some were in charge of guarding the Temple from impurity: And He set
the porters at the gates of the house of God, that none which was unclean
should enter. (2 Chron. 23:19).

- Shallum was the chief porter (gate or doorkeeper) and his name mean
  restore, to pay retribution, to hand out deserved punishment for evil done.
- Akkub was a gatekeeper along with his brother Shallum, Talmon, and
  Ahiman. His name means pursuer, to follow in order to overtake and

capture. Now this gatekeeper is a warrior intercessor, he pursues and doesn't stop until he has accomplish the his mission.

- Talmon/Telem was a gatekeeper, his name mean to break upon or treat violently. We as gatekeeper are not to be chased by the enemy and his demons, but are to pursue and overtake them. Gatekeeper/intercessor are to go after the enemy of our souls with a vengeance using the judgment written which is the sword of the Word.
- Meshelemiah was a gatekeeper responsible for keeping the door of the tabernacle during meeting. He was responsible for allowing people to enter or not enter into the meeting or service, 1 Chronicles 9:21.

Gatekeeper, porter was known also as doorkeeper and there duty was to guard the entrance into a city, public building and or the entrance within a building. They would be stationed at any entrance through which someone unwanted might enter, especially at night. Their primary duties were to serve in the house of the Lord (1 Chron. 26:12). Gatekeeper is also known as watchers. They operate in a different function in the temple. Some were men of great ability (7), able men with strength for the work (8), wise counselors (14), some guarded the storehouse (God's finances), some were watchmen of the highway (14). Some watchmen are given assignments of nation, cities, continents, geographic area, people and place as Daniel and Jeremiah. Some were deliverers and harvester of souls as Moses. The first thing watchmen are given is to be watchmen over their own life and their character. We must have integrity and be true to our words.

What one should know about the office of the gatekeepers?

- It's an chosen office (1 Chronicles 9:22).
- It's an ordained assignment (1 Chronicles 9:23,24).
- It's a responsibility (1 Chronicles 9:27).

Prophetic Watchmen

> So you, son of man: I have made you a watchman for the house of Israel; therefore you shall hear a word from my mouth and warn them for Me (Ezekiel 33:7).

Watchmen watched over cities, harvests, fields stood on the walls at doorways and gates to protected and guard the sanctuary. They watched for enemies and for messengers. They recognized a messenger by (his walk). A good intercessor will recognize wolves by their spiritual walk (2 Samuel 18:19-28).

According the American Standard Exhaustive Concordance, the word watchman comes from the Hebrew "tsaphah" meaning to look out, about, spy and to keep watch. The same root word tsaphah also means to lay out, lay over, outflow or discharge. The word watchman comes from a Hebrew root, meaning to hedge about, to guard, generally to protect and observe from a distance.

The prophetic watchmen duties are:

- To look out, to spy, keep watch over a situation or person, city or nations
- To lay out the need before God.
- To lay over to bring protection to someone or something with prayers.
- To have an outflow or flowing out from the intercessor's spirit to the Spirit of God
- To discharge (as of a burden) from our spirit to God.

The Prophetic watchman has all of the above traits and a more deeper anointing. Many wish to accept the good prophecy but push to the side the prophecy that tell us to stop our mess.

The Prophet with the watchman anointing has the ability to edify, exhort, comfort, chasten/correct, rebuke, reprove, declare, decree and proclaim (1 Cor.14:3; Titus 2:15).

Listed below are the not-so-likeable side of prophetic ministry:

- Edify—To edify means to uplift, build up, instruct and offer hope and improve morals and religious knowledge. In Latin is it means to erect a house.
- Exhort—To exhort means to give urgent advice, to caution, to forewarn, to remind, to counsel and encourage.

Scriptures of exhortation

- Exhorting them to continue in the faith (Acts 14:22).
- Exhort and rebuke with all authority (Titus 2:15).
- Exhort one another daily (Heb. 3:13).
- Comfort—To comfort mean to console in time of trouble or worry, to encourage, to give strength and hope, to make cheerful.

- Correction—To correct mean to set or make right that which is wrong. It implies taking action to remove errors, faults, defects or to bring to conformity to an approved standard.

Scriptures of correction/chasten

- Withhold not correction from the child (Prov. 23:13).
- As many as I love, I rebuke and chasten (Rev. 3:19).
- Chasten—To chasten means "to discipline, purify, correct, restrain, prune of excess"

Scriptures of Chastening

- I will chastise you seven times for your sins (Lev. 26:28).
- I will chasten him with the rod of men (2 Sam. 7:14).
- Despise not thou the chastening of the Almighty (Job 5:17).
- Chasten thy son while there is hope (Prov. 19:18).
- Rebuke—The different between rebuke and reproof is reproof is a kinder way of correcting a fault whereas rebuke is a sharp stern correction. Reprimand is a more severe form of correction and is often done publicly. To rebuke means to sharply reprimand, express strong disapproval, criticize and to check.

Scriptures of Rebuke

- Rebuke a wise man and he will love thee (Prov. 9:8).
- Open rebuke is better than secret love (Prov. 27:5).
- They hate him that rebuketh (Amos 5:10).
- Jesus rebuked the winds (Matt. 8:26).
- Jesus rebuked the devil (Matt. 17:18).
- Jesus rebuked a fever (Luke 4:39).
- Rebuke with all authority (Titus 2:15).
- Rebuke them sharply (Titus 1:13).
- Reproof—Reproof means a softer way of correcting one for there faults.

Scriptures of Reproof

- Reproof and instruction are the way of life (Prov. 6:23).
- He that often reproved hardeneth his neck (Prov. 29:1).

- There backslidings shall reprove thee (Jer. 2:19).
- All scripture are profitable for doctrine, for reproof (2 Tim. 3:16).
- Preach the word, reprove, rebuke (2 Tim. 4:2).
- Warning—According to the Webster's Dictionary warning means to put one on guard, caution, forewarn, notify, advise before it happen, give a signal or sound an alarm that impending danger or evil is about to take place.

Scriptures of Warnings

- Man of God . . . warned Him (2 Kings 6:10).
- Warn them that they trespass not against the Lord (2 Chron. 19:10).
- Blow the trumpet, and warn the people (Ezek. 33:3).
- Warn them that are unruly (1 Thess. 5:14).
- Warn the wicked (Ezek 3:19).
- Warn the wicked of his way to turn from it (Ezek 33:9).

Finally, the prophetic watchmen also have the ability to declare and decree things.

Prophetic Seers

Prophets were in old times called seers (1 Samuel 9:9), so the watchman had to "see" into the spirit what God wants him to see and take authority over forces of spiritual darkness that hold people in bondage to sin and darkness. Because the prophetic watchman is called to see, he peers into the distance and can foretell danger from a distance or can sense imminent danger, 2 Samuel 18:24-27; 2 Kings 9:17-21). There are many seers mention in the scripture such as Heman, the King's seer (1 Chron. 25:5); Hanani, the seer 2 Chr. 19:2; Asaph, the seer 2 Chron. 29:30; Amaziah, the seer Amos 7:12; and Samuel, the seer 1 Sam. 9:19. God said "He revealeth his secret unto his servants the prophets" (Amos 3:7). Just because God reveals you a secret that doesn't mean that you are to share it at that time. Be mindful of God's timing, release and nudging.

The anointing of the watchman originates from the office of the prophet. The prophetic watchman has the ability to speak to principalities, powers, thrones, and dominions and cause them to hear the manifold wisdom of God. When devils are put into their place, spiritual atmospheres change, people change, laws change. Please note, there is an actual shifting in government as a result of the activities of the prophetic watchman. The person who is a prophetic watchman is called by God to fulfill this role. All Christians are called to a lifestyle of prayer and to intercede, but the function of the prophetic intercessors are different from simple intercessor with a prayer anointing. I believe prophetic watchman are prophets and not just intercessors. I further believe that intercessors can flow under a prophetic anointing, which does not make them a prophet.

Guideline to Prophesying

- No prophecy of the scripture is of any private interpretation (2 Pet. 1:20).
- Remember he that prophesy speaketh unto men to edification (1 Cor. 14:3).
- Prophesy according to the preparation of your faith (Romans 12:6).
- Let the Lord put His words in your mouth not you (Ezek. 3:27).

Prophets who are watchmen has the Divine ability to decree and declare God's word for manifestation and breakthrough.

Chapter 11

PROPHETIC DECREES AND DECLARATIONS

You will decree a thing and it will be established for you so
light will shine on your ways.

—Job 22:28

According to Webster's Dictionary "decree" means to give an official order usually having the force/or backing of the law behind it. Its a command. A decree is the turning of events of this world so they come in agreement with God commands and programs. Therefore, it is an authoritative order, directive or command enforced by the law of the land or by heaven. It's a judicial decision from a higher court in our case, the God of heaven. A decree speaks of faith and authority back up by God. Authority means you have the right to exercise power, government authority and have a lawful right to enforce that obedience. When we decree a thing, we're operating in the creative power of God word speaking those things that are not seen to become manifested in the earth realm. We are declaring and decreeing His dominion, His power, His authority, His rule, His Kingdom, His glory to be established on the earth as it is in the heaven. We are calling those thing which be not as though they were Romans 4:17. The spoken word has power and it is enforced by faith. If you can believe it you can have it as long as it is in agreement with the Word. Listen to what Jesus says, I tell you with certainty, if anyone says to this mountain, be lifted up and thrown into the sea, if he doesn't doubt in his heart, but believes that what he says will happen, it will be done for him. Therefore, I say unto you, what things soever you desire, when you pray, believe that you shall have them. (Mark 11:23-24).

Declare means to make evident, to affirm and to make clearly known, state or announce openly, to say positively, to make a statement publicly or officially declared with authority. Remember we have to speak in order to announce something. What are we announcing? We are announcing to ungodly forces that Jesus is Lord and speaking God's word that has preeminence over what we see in the natural and demand it to conform to the spoken and living Word. Jesus said, it is the Spirit who gives life; the flesh accomplishes nothing. The words that I speak are Spirit and life. (John 6:63).

PROCLAMATION

Proclaim is to announce officially and publicly, typically insistently, proudly, or defiantly and in either speech or writing, to give an outward indication of. Therefore, when we speak God's word which is already written and established in the heavens we give them power for being manifested. We enforce the word through what I call a verbal agreement. Jesus said, the words that he speak are spirit and they are life (John 8:32). Words has power to produce either for good or bad. The written word is God's will in a tangible form. Now, what is God's will? God's will is His Word. It is an official order or legal ruling from God effecting change in situations and affairs causing it to come into agreement with His Divine plan.

When the children of Israel was in a fight for there very lives, Queen Esther sent out a decreed and proclaimed a fast for her people and the entire race was saved by an act of obedience.

Listed below are a set of decrees and declarations that I believe will help release the power that's in the word. Read these decrees out loud, speaking in faith and then watch your life takes on new meaning. We would like to begin by placing on the whole armor of God first. It is time to decree, proclaim and declare the things Christ has already completed at the Cross. Remember, to decree or declare a thing, it must be activated by speaking it out and by faith. Be bold and say what the Word is says about our situations. When we declare a thing, we must realize that we have begun a fierce campaign to get rid of something or to start something, to fight for or against something. For instant, if you are sick we began to speak the word I am well even thought you're on medication, speak I am well. Decreeing, proclaiming or declaring is not something to be used lightly and be used every now and then, but are to be spoken until we see the answer or evidence manifest in the natural.

DECREE AND DECLARING KINGDOM PRINCIPLES

Put on the Whole Armor, Romans 13:12; Ephesians 6:13-17

1. We place upon ourselves the Armor of Light.
2. We place on truth to cover my loins (Psalms 51:6).
3. We place on the breastplate of righteousness to cover my heart and chest (Psalms 5:12; 2 Cor. 6:7).
4. We place on the gospel of peace to cover my feet (Isaiah 52:7).
5. We place on the shield of faith to defensively and offensively cover my body (Hebrews 10:38; 11:1, 6).
6. We place on the helmet of salvation to cover my head (1 Thess. 5:8; Isaiah 59:17).
7. We place on the sword of the Spirit, which is the Word of God (Ephesians 6:17; Rev. 1:16).
8. We place on the robe of righteousness (Isaiah 61:10).

God rules
   We DECREE & DECLARE the Most High rules in the Kingdom of men and He gives it to whomever He will and sets over it the lowest of men (Daniel 4:17).
   We DECREE & DECLARE every dominion of the Kingdom of men must tremble and fear before our God for He is the living God. His Kingdom shall not be destroyed; His dominion shall endure to the forever. He is the God that deliver, rescue work signs and wonders in heaven and in earth (Daniel 6:26-27).

The Body of Christ
   We DECREE & DECLARE we are sons and daughters of God no longer strangers and foreigner but citizens with the saints and members of the household faith. We say, sons and daughters of God arise take your rightful place. We are built upon the foundation of the apostles and prophets, Jesus Christ being the chief cornerstone and being joined together growing into a holy temple of the Lord (Psalms 2:7: Ephesians 2:19-22).
   We DECREE & DECLARE that the body of Christ are strengthened in the faith, increased in number daily, Acts 16:5. We say body of Christ bring forth children into the Kingdom of God.

Dress for Battle

We DECREE & DECLARE this day we are strong in the Lord and in the power of His might. We have on the full armor of God and stand against the schemes, plans, trickery, plots of the evil one in every area of our life. We are not fighting against human beings but against spiritual rulers, authorities and cosmic powers of this age in high places (Ephesians 6:10-11).

Word of Truth

We DECREE & DECLARE we stand ready with our minds fastened with the truth of God's Word and faith as our shield to withstand all the burning arrows shot by the evil one. We have on the helmet of salvation and the coat of righteousness (Mark 11:22; Ephesians 6:16; Hebrews 11:1).

Weapons of warfare

We DECREE & DECLARE that the weapons we use in our fight are not the world's weapons but God's powerful weapons to destroy strongholds. We use faith, prayer, intercession, spiritual warfare, holy boldness, confident, fasting, forgiveness, righteousness, goodness, mercy, kindness, steadfastness and above all the love of God. We destroy false arguments, pull down every proud obstacle that is raised against the knowledge of God. We take every evil thought and imagination captive and cause it to become subject to Christ to the laws and mind of God (2 Corinthians 10:4; John 3:16).

DECREEING AND DECLARING FOR A CHOSEN GENERATION

Royal Priesthood

We DECREE & DECLARE we are a chosen generation, a royal priesthood, a holy nation proclaiming the praises of God who has called us out of darkness into His marvelous light of salvation. We decree that we are a people ordained to offer spiritual worship to Him. We are the head and not the tail. We have favor with God and man (1 Pet. 2:2, 9; Luke 2:52; Deut. 28:13).

A Holy and fruitful people

We DECREE & DECLARE truth in the lives of believers. We are a holy people. We decree that we are blessed and multiplying in the thing of God. We say fruit of our womb come forth, barren give birth. Every barren place in our life rise up an produce fruit. We decree and declare that our bodies are healed, sickness be gone for by Christ we are healed. We decree that our heart will not be deceived into worshipping other god (Deut. 7:6, 13-15, 11:16).

Servants of the Most High
We DECREE & DECLARE that we will service the Lord with all our heart, all our soul and with all our might and we shall diligently keep His commandments, testimonies and statutes. We shall do that which is right and good in His sight that it may be well with us in the land we possess (Deut. 6:4, 17-18).

Strong and Courageous
We DECREE & DECLARE we are a people of conquest. We are strong and courageous end-time warriors use as weapon against the enemy; we are prosperous and have good success in all that we set our hands to do. We are the sons and daughters born and led by the Spirit of God (Josh. 1:6-7, 24:15; Romans 8:14; 2 Chron. 11:1).

Peoples of the Spirit
We DECREE & DECLARE we are a people who walk after the spirit of God and not according to the dictates of our flesh. The law of the Spirit of life in Christ has made us free from the law of sin and death. We say sin loose us and let us go. We decree today that we walk in freedom. We're no longer enslaved to the fleshly desires of sexual lusts, outbursts of anger and envy. We chose to walk in the fruit of the spirit of love, peace, kindness, goodness, self-control and faithfulness (Galatians. 5:16, 19, 22; Romans 8:2).

Anointed Heirs
We DECREE & DECLARE that we are the children, heirs and joint heirs with Christ. Each day we are being transformed into the sons of God, whom He foreknew and predestined to be conformed to His image and in according to His purpose. We decree that we walk by faith and not by what we see (Romans 8:16, 18, 28-29; 2 Cor. 5:7; Psalms 37:23).

A righteous people
We DECREE & DECLARE that we are the righteous of God in Christ Jesus and walk in mercy, tenderness and humility. We decree that we have

been delivered from the power of darkness and translated into the Kingdom of God. We are good stewards of the Gospel. We trust in the Lord with our whole heart and lean not upon our own understanding. In all our ways we acknowledge Him, and He directs our paths, (2 Cor. 5:7; Colossians 1:13; 1 Peter 4:10; Prov. 3:5-6).

New Creation

We DECREE & DECLARE the old worldly lifestyles are passed away and we are a new creation in Christ. We do not focus on the things we once did but move forward with a renewed mind in the things of Christ and the things that's eternal. The things which are seen are temporary, but the things which are not seen are eternal. We are citizen of Heaven. (2 Cor. 4, 18, 5:17).

The mind of Christ

We DECREE & DECLARE we're not high-minded we have the mind of Christ and are being transformed in His image day by day. For it is God who works in us, both to do His will and do His good pleasure. We commit our works to Him and our thoughts are established (Phil. 2:5,12:3:21;16:3).

Kingdom increasing

We DECREE & DECLARE that God's Kingdom and His government is increasing. We increase in wisdom, strength and favor (Luke 2:52; Isaiah 9:7).

DECREEING AND DECLARING SPIRITUAL EMPOWERMENT

Spiritual recharge

We DECREE & DECLARE we are edified and recharged by the spirit as we pray in our heavenly language which help up to build our faith. Our spirit is stirred to do Your will (Hag. 1:14; Jude 1:20; 1 Cor. 14:4).

Weapons of Warfare

We DECREE & DECLARE the weapons of our warfare are not carnal, or of a worldly nature but mighty through God to pull down strongholds, casting down vain imaginations and every high thing that lifts itself against the knowledge of the Word. We decree and declare that the name of the Lord is our weapon (2 Cor. 10:3-6, 1; Samuel 17:45).

Anointed power

We DECREE & DECLARE God's anointing destroys every yoke in our lives, soul, spirit and body and we now function in divine order according to God's divine systems of protocol (1 Cor. 9, 27, 14:40).

Obedience to the Spirit's stirring

We DECREE & DECLARE we are obedient to the prompting, stirring, leading and insight of the Holy Spirit because He make intercession for us with unspeakable words. We walk in the spirit of excellent (Romans. 8:26; Daniel 6:3).

The Spirit of the Lord rests upon the righteous

We DECREE & DECLARE the Spirit of the Lord is upon us, the spirit of righteousness, spirit of wisdom, spirit of quick understanding, the spirit of divine counsel, the spirit of supernatural might, the spirit of knowledge and the utmost fear of the Lord. As we advance and are divinely empowered with God's strength we will continue to increase in skills and understanding (Isaiah 11:2-3; Colossians 1:9-11, 3:10; Ephesians 1:17-18; Phil. 1:11).

DECREEING AND DECLARING DIVINE HEALING FOR SICKNESS

Healing

We DECREE & DECLARE the Most High is bring healing, miraculous deliverance and total restoration to our family, children, extended family, friends and our nation to establish a testimony for His name. We decree this proclamation goes into effect this day and the enemy must obey and release them now. Father hasten your Word to perform it (Jeremiah 1:12).

Sickness and disease

We DECREE & DECLARE that our bodies are healed by Jesus' stripes. The Lord heals all our diseases. No sickness or plague will come near my dwelling for we are redeemed from sickness and disease and every plague is stopped when it comes near us (Gal. 3:13; Ps. 91:10, 103:3; Isaiah 53:5; Num. 16:50).

DECREEING AND DECLARING VICTORY FOR MEN

A man of wisdom

We DECREE & DECLARE I am a man of wisdom that thirst for God with my whole heart. I am filled with wisdom, insight and understanding. Therefore, I understand my purpose and walk in the Spirit and as your Word order my steps. I am able to discern matters, both natural, spiritual and weight them by your word. My expectation shall not be cut short or off for my trust is in the Lord (Eccl. 7:19).

Man of faith

We DECREE & DECLARE we are forgiving men, faithful servant and good steward of God's word. We decree God's laws are hidden in our heart and produces fruit on a daily basis. We decree that the Word is stored in our heart spring forth and produce mature fruit. Because of the God we choose to do right. We are not easily offended; your law governs our body, soul and spirit. We walk uprightly with a heart of faith, for we are the salt and light of the world and we always do those things that are pleasing to you (Col. 3:13; Matt. 6:14, 15).

Men thirsty for God

We DECREE & DECLARE we thirst for you like a deer in need of water. Teach us how to seek you when we are in a dry and weary place. We hear your voice Lord and walk accordingly. Our heart is captivated by You. Heal the hidden places in our heart, Psalms. 42:1.

DECREEING AND DECLARING HEALTHY RELATIONSHIP

Marriage

We DECREE & DECLARE all schemes and plans against godly marriage are thwarted in the Name of Jesus. No weapon formed against godly marriage shall prosper for we are of one heart, mind and will. Love in marriages are growing, expanding and flowing like a mighty river. We decree there is no division between husbands and wives. We are rooted and grounded in God's love. We decree that husbands are the head of the home and a great provider for the family. We decree that wives are kind, intelligent, respectful, virtuous women and will do their husband good all the days of their life. We decree that our wives are precious jewels, full of value and worth (Col. 3:18, 19; Prov. 31:1-31).

Wife

We DECREE & DECLARE our husbands are godly men full of the Holy Spirit. They are kind and considered. They are full of tenderness and merciful. They are loving fathers, who trains their children in the things of God's word. Peace rules their heart. They are diligent workers, forgiving and loving, faithful and good steward of their homes. They are loving and not bitter (Col. 3:12-13, 19).

Husband

We DECREE & DECLARE our wives are building our household, they have a charming, gentle and quiet spirit. They are pearls of great price and full of wisdom. They are great helpmate fitly joined together with us for a perfect match. Our wives are respectful and care for our children. They are fruitful in every good work and increasing in the knowledge of God (Col. 2:10, 3:19).

DECREEING AND DECLARING BLESSINGS

Increase in plenty

We DECREE & DECLARE that we honor the Lord with the first fruits of all our increase so shall our barns be filled with plenty. The wealth of the sinner is stored up for the righteous and is being released into our hands now. Every assignment of the enemy against our finances are broken. We say money come from the north, south, east and west (Prov. 3:9-10, 13:22).

Overtaking blessing

We DECREE & DECLARE because we diligently obey God's voice and observe carefully all His commandments He will bless us. We decree a release of the blessings of the Lord be upon us and overtaking us. We decree we are blessed in the city, Blessed is the fruit of our body. We say basket be blessed and filled. We're blessed when we come into a place and when we go out. The blessings are commanded by the Lord upon us in the storehouses and all that we set out hands to do are greatly blessed. We decree that we are lenders and shall lend to many nations and not borrow (Deut. 28:2-8, 12).

Showers of blessing
We DECREE & DECLARE showers of blessing is coming daily and our barns are full and overflowing. The Lord command His blessing upon our property and we eat and are satisfied. We decree that we are brought into a good land without scarceness and lack (Ezek. 34:26; Prov. 3:10; Deut. 28:8; Psalms 144:13-14; Joel 2:26; Deut. 8:9).

Blessing at the gates
We DECREE & COMMAND blessings to come from the north gate, the south gate, east gate and west gate, be open in our city (Isaiah 60:11).

Kingdom builders
We DECREE & DECLARE we are Kingdom builders. And we press into the Kingdom. Let our gates be opened continually to receive your blessings (Isaiah 60:11).

Blessing of durable riches
We DECREE & DECLARE honor, durable riches and righteousness are with us. He has given us the ability to inherit substance and our treasures are filled we say silver be plenteous and fill our house. We are blessed and our borders are enlarged. Wealth and riches are in our house and our righteousness endures forever (Psalms. 91:16; Deut. 12:20; Job 28:1; Prov. 8:18, 21).

Blessing of wealth and riches
We DECREE & DECLARE God takes pleasure in the prosperity of His people. We decree that curses of poverty, lack, debt are broken from our lives for the Lord teaches us how to prosper (Psalms 35:27, 112:1).

Giving good measures blessing
We DECREE & DECLARE as we give men shall give to us in good measure, pressed down, shaken together and running over. We decree we have no hole in our purse and the devourer is rebuked for our sake (Mal. 3:10-11; Hag. 1:6).

Prosperity blessing

We DECREE & DECLARE prosperity is sent from the Lord daily He had dealt bountifully to us giving His good treasures in its season. We decree that we are the head and not the tail, above only and not beneath because we listen and carefully observe His laws (Psalms 119:17, 118:25; Deut. 28:13).

Hidden treasures

We DECREE & DECLARE the treasures gates are open and we go in and receive the treasure of darkness and hidden riches from their secret places. Break the gates of brass and cut in sunder the bars of iron that tried to hinder our treasures release. The gates of hell cannot prevail against us (Matt. 16:18; Isaiah 45:1-3).

DECREEING AND DECLARING PURPOSE AND ASSIGNMENTS

Born for purpose

We DECREE & DECLARE we are born for a divine purpose. Before God formed us in the belly He knew us, before we came forth out of the womb He sanctified us and ordained us for service. He set us over the nations and over the Kingdoms to root out, pull down, to destroy, to throw down, to build and plant (Jer. 1:5, 10; Psalms. 5:12, 37:23; Isaiah 66:9).

Set times and seasons

We DECREE & DECLARE our set times, seasons and purpose are in the hands of the Lord and they shall not be altered or adjusted by anyone or anything. We declare that we function under the anointing of the Sons of Issachar and God gives us the divine ability to accurately discern our times and seasons. He reveals the deep and secret things to us for we are wise and have understanding hearts. We will know what we ought to do at our set times, seasons and purpose (1 Chron. 12:32; Psalms 31:15; Eccles. 3:1-8; Dan. 2:21-22).

Uniting our hearts with God

We DECREE & DECLARE our hearts are united with God's heart to fear His name. Our hearts are fixed, we will accomplish our ordained assignment and will live to declare the works of the Lord. We will be of good courage and strength in our heart (Psalms 31:24, 86:11, 108:1, 118:17).

Divine agenda

We DECREE & DECLARE that this day we operate according to God's divine timetable/calendar. We decree that God's agenda is our agenda we are not our own. We have been bought with a price. We decree that our set time is here now and we move according to God's set time for our life (Psalms. 40:7, 139:16; 1 Cor. 7:23; James 4:7).

Good and fruitful works

We DECREE & DECLARE God has began a good work in us and will complete it. We are fruitful in every good work and increasing in the knowledge of God (Phil. 1:6; Col. 1:10).

DECREEING AND DECLARING SPIRITUAL INSIGHT

Spiritual vision

We DECREE & DECLARE the eyes of our are spirit functioning with 20/20 vision for correct understanding and interpretation of the divine movements. Our ears are in tune to the correct frequency of the Spirit to know what God is saying and we have clear transmission and will receive the things that are in the heaven realm for us (2 Corinthians 4:4; Psalms 119:18; Jer. 1:11-16; Ephesians 4:18; 2 Kings 6:17; Job 42:5; Rev. 4:1).

Floodgates of heaven opened

We DECREE & DECLARE the floodgates of heaven are opened over our life and God shows us His visions and revelation. We decree secret and deep things are revealed and we understand the hidden things by the Spirit of God (Mat. 13:35; Mal. 3:10; Ezek. 1:1; Dan. 2:2.2).

Revelation of purpose

We DECREE & DECLARE that we have sound understand of our purpose for this life and know it through by the Spirit. The mysteries of the Kingdom are revealed to us now. (Deut. 29:29; 1 Cor. 14:6; Mark 4:11).

Abundance revelations

We DECREE & DECLARE God's righteousness is revealed unto us. We receive sound wisdom from Him and decree the manifestation of abundant revelations to come forth and enlighten our heart (2 Cor. 12:1; Isaiah 56:1).

Feet firmly planted

We DECREE & DECLARE that our feet are firmly planted in the house of the Lord we will not be shaken and are always flourishing in His courts. We are planted by the rivers of water and our roots has grown deep and we will not be moved. We declare that we will bring forth fruit in our old age. Your covenant with us will not be broken nor will the things be alter from your lips which you have said concerning us, (Psalms 89:34, 92:13-14).

The love of God

We DECREE & DECLARE nothing will separate us from the love of God and the Gospel of light will continued to flood our heart day and night until our mind are renewed. We are seated in heavenly places with Christ, far above all powers and dominions and powers; therefore, I will not look to the natural but to the spiritual for help.

DECREEING AND DECLARING GUIDANCE

Steps ordered

We DECREE & DECLARE that our steps are ordered and established by God and He delight in our ways. As the righteous, we are blessed, favored and greatness is our portion (Psalms 37:23).

Guidance

We DECREE & DECLARE that God guide us into all truth for His name's sake and He guide our affairs with discretion (Psalms. 31:3; Isaiah. 58:11, 112:5).

Making crooked places straight

We DECREE & DECLARE that crooked places are made straight and the rough places made smooth before us. Light and truth is sent to lead us in a plain path and we are delivered from the evil one (Psalms. 43:3; Isaiah. 40:4; Matt. 6:13).

DECREEING AND DECLARING ANGELIC PROTECTION

Deliverance

We DECREE & DECLARE the Lord have delivered our soul from death and our feet from falling. He has given His angels to encamp around us to deliver us. We decree that we are delivered and set free from the enemy's every invisible and visible trap, plan, snare and net assigned to us. The Lord's Angels guard, protect and deliver us in the night season (Psalms 33:7, 116:8; Acts 12:6).

Divine angelic undertakings

We DECREE & DECLARE that successful divine, angelic undertakings, undergirding, reinforcements and divine assistance be given to the righteous in every area of their life, home and ministry. We decree a hedge of divine protection surrounds us at all times, according to your word in Psalm 103:20, angels now excel in strength to marshal and protect our person, property and possession (2 Kings 6:17; Daniel 3:15-30; Acts 12:1-10).

Angels Divine ministers

We DECREE & DECLARE angels are to minister on our behalf. They are released to fight for our defend; they are released to war against any spirit in the heavens assigned to block our prayers from being answered. We say angels of the Living God rise up and fight. (Mat. 4:11; Psalms. 68:17; Acts 27:23; Daniel 10:12-13).

Forgiveness

We DECREE & DECLARE that we have not hidden our sins and iniquities, but acknowledged them. You said if we acknowledge and forsake them You would forgive. We decree our hearts have been washed thoroughly from our iniquities, sins and have been cleaned by the blood of Jesus Christ. Thank you for forgiving our sins. (Psalms 32:5, 51:2-3, 10).

DECREEING AND DECLARING DIVINE SAFETY

Angelic protection

We DECREE & DECLARE that your angels have charge over us to deliver us from our enemies. They are fighting for us in the heavens against principalities and making crooked places straight that our way may prosper (Daniel 10:13; Psalms 91:11; Zech. 12:13).

Divine protection

We DECREE & DECLARE that we dwell in the secret place of the most High and abide under the shadow of the Almighty. He is our refuge and fortress for we trust in Him. Surely He shall deliver us from the snare of the fowler from noisome pestilence and shalt cover us with His feathers, under His wings shall we trust. His truth shall be our shield and buckler. We shall not be afraid of the terror by night nor the arrow that flie by day, nor of pestilence that walk in darkness, nor destruction that wasteth at noonday a thousand shall fall at thy side and ten thousand at the right hand, but it shall not come nigh thee. There shall no evil befall us neither shall any plague come nigh our dwelling. He shall give his angels charge over us to keep us in all our ways. And the angels shall bear us up in their hands lest we dash our foot against a stone. For He has set His love upon us therefore shall we be delivered (Psalms. 91:1-16).

Gates of righteousness
We DECREE & DECLARE the gates of righteousness are opened and we enter through them praising the Lord with a thankful heart. This is the day the Lord has made and we will rejoice and be glad in it (Psalms. 100:4, 118:19, 24).

Worshippers
We DECREE & DECLARE that we are passionate worshippers that worship in spirit and in truth (John 4:23).

Faith walkers
We DECREE & DECLARE that we are faith walkers and we walk not by what we see (2 Corinthians 5:7).

Salt Seasoners
We DECREE & DECLARE that believers are the salt that season the human race. We are lights that shine in the darkness of people's lives and they see the good things we do and praise the Father (Mat. 5:13-14).

Givers
We DECREE & DECLARE that we are givers and not takers. We give generously to the needy and His kindness shall never fail us (Psalms 112:9).

DECREEING AND DECLARING FOR SPIRITUAL WARFARE

Works of Satan
We DECREE & DECLARE Satan's kingdom and works are destroyed and they must come down for this is the purpose for which

Jesus was manifested. For all kingdoms are the Lord's and He rules over the nations. The Heavens declare the glory of God and the firmament shows His handiwork. God is Lord of everything. Therefore, Satan, your kingdom must come down (Psalms. 19:1, 22:28; John 3:8; Isaiah 14:13-14; Ezek. 28:2).

Divided Kingdom

We DECREE & DECLARE that Satan's kingdom is continuingly being divided against itself and brought to desolation and it shall utterly fall, your armed palace and goods are snatched from you and the spoils are divided. We decree that you walk through dry places seeking rest and finding none we bar you from your previous home forever and we close every door that will cause our lives to be a revolving door (Luke 11:17-18, 21-22, 24, 26).

Releasing legal rights

We DECREE & DECLARE that we break all legal right and curses causing you to operate leave now. All ungodly forces and activities ruling over nations, government, states, families, children, godly relationship causing discord, broken marriages be loose from your assignment. We command that you stop and desist; we release you from your assignment now and ask Father to send godly angels to rule in your places (Gal. 3:13; Matt. 18:18; 2 Corinthians 4:4).

Overtake the enemy

We DECREE & DECLARE the enemy of our soul is being overtaken and consumed as we speak, wounded and not able to rise again. They fall under the feet of Jesus and are crushed and we decree the gates of hell will not prevail against us in Jesus' name (Psalms. 18:37-38, 91:13; Matt. 16:18).

Binding the Prince

We decree and declare that the prince of the power of the air, wickedness in high places are bound (Ephesians 2:2, 12; 2 Cor. 4:4).

DECREEING AND DECLARING VICTORY OVER THE CONTINENTS

Binding and releasing Salvation

We bind Principles, Power, Rulers of darkness and Wicked Spirits over the continents to hinder salvation. Over the continents of North America,

South America, Europe, Africa, Asia, Australia we say open your ears to receive the Gospel. We command these regions to open. We bind every ungodly purpose designed to destroy, influence, seduce people, leaders and key person in authority over these areas. We say that the undermining forces be uprooted by God angelic powers. We decree forces of deception, power struggle be broken, diabolical alliance be separate and destroyed. We nullify the power of any sacrifice made to devils in these continents in Jesus's Name (Ephesians 4; Lev. 17:7; Mat.12:28-29, 16:19).

Assignments fulfilled

We DECREE & DECLARE that nations are being set free; strongholds are broken in the name of Jesus Christ. We declare and decree all materials used to construct strongholds in our lives, homes, environment, communities, cities, country, nations, and the world are now demolished and utterly destroyed. So we might live in peace. We ask that angels go and totally annihilate and crush to dust every stronghold. We decree and declare that mercy and truth meet together, righteousness and peace kiss each other, righteousness look down from heaven and let truth spring out of the earth. We say, land yield your increase. Let the harvest of souls for Jesus come forth in abundant (Psalms 85:10-13; Mat. 9:37).

Pulling down Strongholds

- We DECREE & DECLARE that the weapons of our warfare are not carnal, but mighty through God to the pulling down of strongholds (2 Cor. 10:4).

Fulfillment of assignments

- We DECREE & DECLARE that Geographical assignments are fulfilled. And God's word is covering Geographical area as the water cover the sea (Mark 5:1-10).
- Cultural assignments are fulfilled (Num. 33:50-55).
- Individual assignments are fulfilled (1 Sam. 28:3-9; 1 Chron.10:13). We lose people in these regions from the spirit of error, the wrong spirit in Jesus' name.
- We decree that floodgates of salvation are open to all regions (Luke 9:55; 1 John 4:6).

Prophetic Proclamations

Prophetic proclamations are given through the inspiration of the Holy Spirit to verbally declare God's will in a given situation.

Example: We proclaim that God's will be done in nations of the world and souls will be saved. Your word declares that every knee shall bow and every tongue shall declare that you are Lord. We say, will of God be done and doors of utterance be open for the Gospel entrance.

Chapter 12

RESISTING AND PREVAILING
IN THE KINGDOM

What does resisting mean? Resist mean to stand your ground, to put up a fight, James 4:7 says, "Resist the devil and he will flee." Ephesians 6:13 says, Stand your ground". Resisting has to do with being alert, standing firm in the faith submit to God and have on the armor of God. If you do not have these you will not be able to resist the enemy. In resisting the enemy we must have the following three area covered and walking in righteousness. Let's look at the word prevailing which means to be greater in strength and influence, to win out or over. Not only are we to resist, stand our ground, but to win in the situation. Listed below are some situations we are to resist and prevail over.

We forcefully resist the lies of the devil and prohibit the hijacking of divine thoughts, inspiration, revelation, insight, wisdom, knowledge and understanding emanating from the throne room of our Heavenly Father, especially those that initiate, stimulate, sustain and reinforce Kingdom authority in the earth, in the heaven and facilitate God's redemptive purpose (Ephesians 6:11; Mat.13:19).

We forcefully resist and halt all distractive, disturbing and destructive measures of the enemy to sabotage the Body of Christ in every area of ministry. We decree that the Body of Christ will fulfill their ordained assignment in the earth. We put a halt to every spirit assigned to undermined and destroy covenant relationship, undermined and abort the divine purpose and will of God for a ministry. We say the enemy efforts, plans, influence, all disturbing and destructive measures have been nullified, broken in Jesus Name and are being made evident in the earth realm (1 John 3:8; 2:15-17; Acts 16:16-19).

We forcefully halt, prevail and destroy through the spirit of Christ any satanic inhibitions, prohibitions and all limitations. We decree and declare that all invisible and invincible forces of the enemy are destroyed in our home, town, cities, states, nations and in the world. We command all invisible and invincible forces of witchcraft, astrology, psychics, charmers, enchantment, lies of the devil, seduction, divorce, separation and character assassination become null and void in Jesus' Name. We nullify your powers and effects. Father, let your divine judgment be against these forces and activities warring against them now for our good (Colossians 1:16; Josh. 6:1).

We forcefully bind, halt and dispossess master spirits from their geographical territory, culture, nations, communities, families, ministries and cancel your assignments. Father employ Michael, archangels and the angelic host to handle any satanic contentions, disputes, strivings and resistance concerning orders stated above (Daniel 3:24-25; 6:22, 10:13; Hebrew 1:14; Psalms 91:11, 103:20; 2 Chron. 32:21; 2 Kings 7:5-7).

We forcefully prohibit and block satanic gatekeepers access to individual, family, community, nation, organization or ministry to keep them in bondage. You will no longer steal, kill, or destroy in our city. For we secure the hedge of protection around them and close any illegal entrance (Psalms 24:7-10).

We break diabolical confederations of demons forces assigned, plans and purposes over our churches, ministry, family, communities, nations, leave now, in Jesus Name. We halt the mobilizing of other principalities and spirits that try to help them reform stronger alliances (Acts 16:12-24; Mark 5:1-20; Psalms 83:1-8).

Recommended Reading & Notes

Alves, Elizabeth. Becoming a Prayer Warrior, Ventura, Calif: Renew Books, 1998

Grudem, Wayne. The Gift of Prophecy in the New Testament and Today. Westchester, Il; Crossway Books, 1988

Hamon, Bill. Prophets and Personal Prophecy. Shippensburg, Pa: Destiny Image Publishers, 1987

Resources By

Ora Holloway

Books

Encounters: A Spiritual Journey of Self Confrontations
Facing the issues and struggles within ones personal life $14.00

Glory Stealers: Worship

How to activate and release the presence of God $12.00

Who Was I? Where Was I? Before My Birth? $10.00
Reveals God's Divine purpose and plan for your life

CDs

Its Just A Test—An exciting soul stirring tape $10.00
Faith As We Know It—Is Under Attack $10.00

To order, write to this address:

Touching Lives Outreach Ministry
PO Box 594 Joliet, Il 60434

Made in the USA
Middletown, DE
08 November 2017